THE TRANSFORMATION OF THE POLISH ARMED FORCES: PREPARING FOR NATO

DR PAUL LATAWSKI

The Royal United Services Institute for Defence Studies

First Published 1999

© The Royal United Services Institute for Defence Studies

All rights reserved. No part of this publication may be reproduced, stored in a retrieval system, or transmitted in any form or by any means, electronic, mechanical, photocopying, recording or otherwise, without prior permission of the Royal United Services Institute for Defence Studies.

ISBN   0-85516-106-X
ISSN   0268-1307

The Royal United Services Institute for Defence Studies (RUSI) is an independent professional body based in London dedicated to the study, analysis and debate of issues affecting defence and international security.

Founded in 1831 by the Duke of Wellington, the RUSI is one of the most senior institutes of its kind in the world which, throughout its history, has been at the forefront of contemporary political-military thinking through debates, public and private seminars, conferences, lectures and a wide range of publications. The independence of the Institute is guaranteed by a large, worldwide membership of those people and organisations who have a serious and professional interest in the thorough and objective analysis of defence and international security.

Critical and acclaimed analysis of issues of the moment has underwritten the RUSI's Whitehall Papers for many years. Whitehall Papers are available as part of a membership package, or individually at £6.50 plus p&p (£1.00 in the UK/£2.00 overseas). Orders should be sent to the Publications Department, RUSI Whitehall, London SW1A 2ET UK and cheques made payable to the RUSI. Orders can also be made quoting credit card details (except American Express) via e-mail to: **defence@rusids.demon.co.uk**
For more details, visit our Website: www.rusi.org/rusi/

Printed in Great Britain by Sherrens Printers, Units 1 & 2, South Park, Granby Industrial Estate, Weymouth, Dorset for The Royal United United Services Institute for Defence Studies, Whitehall, London SW1A 2ET UK
Registered Charity No. 210639

CONTENTS

Acknowledgements	iv
Note on the Author	v
Introduction	1
Chapter One Dismantling the Legacy of the Warsaw Pact	4
Chapter Two Painful but Necessary Adjustment: Manpower Issues and Infrastructure	18
Chapter Three Definitive Reform?: Plan 2012	37
Conclusion	61

ACKNOWLEDGEMENTS

This project was greatly aided by the support and encouragement of a number of people. First of all, my thanks go out to Rear Admiral Richard Cobbold, the Director of RUSI, to Dr Jonathan Eyal, the Director of Studies and other members of the RUSI team. In particular Ms Ingeborg Bleken of the editorial department has been very helpful and efficient in addressing technical queries when this paper was in preparation. I extend my warm thanks to individuals in Poland who kindly gave time for interviews during my research trips to Poland: Mr Janusz Onyszkiewicz, the Polish Defence Minister, Dr Andrzej Karkoszka, former First Deputy Defence Minister and Dr Henryk Szlajfer of the policy planning department of the Polish Foreign Ministry. Special thanks go out to Mr Pawel Swieboda of the Presidential Chancellery who kindly arranged interviews and Professor Wojciech Roszkowski, the Director of the Institute for Political Studies, Polish Academy of Sciences who has so kindly offered research facilities and congenial company during my visits to Warsaw. In London, my thanks go out to Captain I Goreczny, the Polish Defence Attaché who patiently answered my queries for information. Finally, the largest thanks go out to my wife for her patience and encouragement during the preparation of this paper.

The opinions expressed in this paper are those of the author and do not necessarily reflect those of either Royal Military Academy Sandhurst or the Ministry of Defence.

NOTE ON THE AUTHOR

Dr Paul Latawski is a Senior Lecturer in the Defence and International Affairs Department, Royal Military Academy Sandhurst. He is also an Associate Fellow in the European Security Programme at the Royal United Services Institute for Defence Studies and an Honorary Visiting Fellow at the School of Slavonic and East European Studies, University of London. His research interests concern security and defence issues in the former communist states of Central and Eastern Europe. He has published widely on these topics.

INTRODUCTION

Since the early 1990s, the centrepiece of Polish security policy has been to obtain membership in Nato. With this goal realised in 1999, it is appropriate to consider how Poland's Armed Forces have been preparing for this event. The Polish Armed Forces bring to the Atlantic Alliance a long and honourable military tradition. The last time that the Polish Armed Forces fought alongside many of the countries that now belong to the Alliance was in the Second World War. In Britain, there is a sense of respect and admiration for the 'gallant Poles', as Winston Churchill called them, because of their wartime air, land and naval efforts alongside British and Commonwealth forces. After 1945, however, the Polish Armed Forces came under the control of the Soviet Union. Soviet military models thus became the dominant and all-pervasive influence to shape the armed forces. This legacy forms the inescapable backdrop of the military reform of post-communist Poland. Since 1989, the Polish armed forces have been endeavouring to shed this Soviet legacy to restore national military ethos and to prepare for membership in the Atlantic Alliance.

The effort to transform the Polish Armed Forces has taken place in the context of a rock-solid consensus in terms of elite and public support for membership in Nato. A survey of the policies of Polish political parties at the time of the Autumn 1997 Parliamentary elections indicated a unanimous view in favour of joining the Alliance among all the major parties with only some reservations expressed by minor parties. These reservations, however, concerned the pace of integration into Nato and not its desirability.[1] Elite opinion in favour of Nato membership for Poland has been more than matched by public support. Between 1993 and 1996, public support in Poland has been growing and in January 1996 an opinion poll indicated that 72 per cent of respondents favouring Nato membership.[2] Opinion polls taken in June 1997, December 1997 and May 1998 indicate that this support has stayed high at 80 per cent, 76 per cent and 74 per cent respectively.[3] Polling within the military has indicated high levels of support among the group most directly affected by Nato membership.[4]

The solidity of public support is best measured by the willingness to pay for additional costs associated with Alliance membership. Although the percentage of support tends to drop over the issue of cost of membership, a majority of the public is still willing to pay more for any additional defence costs that come with joining the Alliance.[5] An added indication of public support in defence matters is the fact that approval of the armed forces as an institution has topped poll ratings for a very long time.[6] If all that the armed forces needed to prepare for Nato were public approbation, then its ability to operate in the Alliance would have been long assured. Unfortunately, turning a broad national consensus on Poland's goal of joining Nato into a concrete programme of military reform has been a daunting prospect.

It is not the intention here to examine the politics of defence in Poland since 1989. Such issues as civil-military relations, questions of parliamentary versus executive pre-eminence in shaping policy and the twists and turns of party politics are beyond the parameters of this study. Successive governments have grappled with the myriad of problems of transition relating to defence with a mixed record. Each of them in any case has endeavoured to achieve the following aim regarding the armed forces as stated by the current Polish Premier, Jerzy Buzek:

> 'Our borders must be safeguarded by an apolitical, competently led army under civilian control. To achieve this aim, we will create a National System of State Defence and increase outlays for the modernisation of the army. We will continue and intensify actions to bring the Polish armed forces up to the requirements of Poland's Nato membership.'[7]

Introduction

The purpose of this Whitehall Paper is to investigate how successful Polish efforts have been to reform the armed forces to meet 'the requirements of Poland's Nato membership'. In doing so, it will concentrate on three broad areas. The first will look at the efforts to dismantle the legacy of the Warsaw Pact in order to provide a new basis upon which to develop the armed forces. The second will examine the retrenchment and restructuring of military personnel and the shaping of its infrastructure to meet the needs of smaller armed forces in Nato. The third will consider the problem of modernisation of the armed forces by looking at the evolution of its post-Cold War force structure, its re-equipment needs and the resources available to meet the cost of these procurement programmes.

NOTES

1. 'Mala sciagawka dla wyborcy '97', *Polityka*, 20 September 1997 and 'Wybor Polski', Wprost, 21 September 1997.
2. 'Polish Attitudes Toward Poland's Integration with Nato, Findings Based on CBOS Polls, 1993-1996', Public Opinion Research Centre (CBOS), Warsaw, April 1996.
3. Opinion poll by CBOS, 15-18 June 1997 in Report by Polish News Agency PAP, opinion poll by Demoskop 4-9 December 1997 in *Rzeczpospolita*, 21-22 February 1998 and opinion poll by Centre for Market Research May 1998 in *Rzeczpospolita*, 30-31 May 1998.
4. Tadeusz Mitek, 'Aprobata warunkowa', *Polska Zbrojna*, 20 February 1998.
5. The cost issue may grow in importance now that Poland has joined the Alliance. See opinion poll by Demoskop 4-9 December 1997 and opinion poll by Pentor Public Opinion Research Centre, September 1997 in Report by PAP News Agency, 15 December 1997.
6. Its recent slide in apparent popularity has been due to the fact that the fire brigade and health service have been added to the institutions listed in the survey changing the spread of the results but still leaving the armed forces in high public esteem. See opinion poll by CBOS, 12-13 December 1998 in *Gazeta Wyborcza*, 29 December 1998.
7. Exposé by Prime Minister Jerzy Buzek to the Sejm, 10 November 1997 in Materials and Documents, 10-11/1997.

Chapter One

Dismantling the Legacy of the Warsaw Pact

The Polish People's Army

Prior to 1989, the Polish armed forces were an integral part of the Warsaw Treaty Organisation (Warsaw Pact). The historical roots of the then People's Army (*Ludowe Wojsko Polskiego*—LWP) lay in the Polish military formations organised under the aegis of the Soviet Union during the Second World War. What started as a division of the infantry in 1943 finished the war at army strength and possessing the cadre of the post-war LWP.[1] Throughout the Second World War and well into the mid-1950s, Soviet officers seconded to the Polish People's Army accounted for a significant percentage of its officer corps. The most prominent example of the Soviet presence in the armed forces was Marshal Konstantin Rokossovskii who served as Defence Minister between 1949 and 1956. His presence was an important measure in that period of Soviet mistrust of its Polish ally and the desire to shape the LWP into a reliable instrument of Soviet policy.[2] The result of this historical legacy could be measured by the pervasive influence of Soviet training, doctrine, force structures and equipment on the development of the Polish People's Army.

By the late 1980s, the Polish Armed Forces evolved into a heavily mechanised force that was designed to participate in and support a Soviet attack on Western Europe. Warsaw Pact operational requirements led to the extensive development of Polish military infrastructure in the western half of the country. The two western military districts (Pomeranian and Silesian) contained about 80 per cent of the

Chapter One: Dismantling the Legacy of the Warsaw Pact

LWP with the remainder in the Warsaw military district covering the eastern half of the country. Although numerous, the Polish armoured vehicle fleet was not necessarily at the cutting edge of technology. The Soviet Union's Warsaw Pact allies were not always the recipients of the most up-to-date Soviet weapon systems and Poland was not an exception to this pattern. Probably only a small portion of the LWP was sufficiently up-to-date to participate in first echelon operations. Apart from providing mechanised cannon-fodder, the LWP's mission was to maintain lines of communications through Poland to Soviet forces in the German Democratic Republic. This meant that the LWP acquired a huge and highly competent engineering capability in such areas as bridging rivers in order to facilitate the movement of Soviet reinforcements westward in the event of war. Another Polish 'specialisation' within the Warsaw Pact was to prepare for an amphibious assault against Denmark. This mission meant that the most prominent feature of the Polish navy was its large inventory of amphibious assault ships while the army maintained an elite 'blue beret' amphibious assault division.

The manpower of the Polish Armed Forces made it the second largest contributor to the Warsaw Pact. In 1989, the armed forces numbered just over 406 000 men. Patterned on Soviet models, the structure of LWP manpower consisted mostly of a mix of professional officers and conscripts. Non-commissioned and warrant officers were substantially lower in number than officers and had a far less significant role than their counterparts in a Nato army. Augmenting this massive army were the Soviet forces of the Northern Group based in Poland. On the basis of a bilateral agreement signed in December 1956, the Soviet Union was able to station in Poland a maximum of 66 000 troops although, in practice, the troop ceiling never exceeded 58 000. Most of the Soviet installations and troops were located in the western half of Poland.[3]

Throughout its almost half century of existence, the armed forces of communist Poland were at best a nationally autonomous rather than a truly sovereign national military organisation. The LWP was effectively an extension of the Soviet armed forces in the framework of the Warsaw Pact. Although its officer corps was made national after 1956 with the departure of the majority of seconded Soviet officers, membership in the Polish United Workers' Party and the elaborate bureaucratic machinery of political control in the form of the Main Political Department *(Glowny Zarzad Polityczny*—GZP) insured reliability. Indeed, the LWP's participation in operations against Czechoslovakia in August 1968 along with successive interventions in domestic upheaval—most notably with martial law in 1980-1981—demonstrated its reliability in service of communism.[4] The longevity of the LWP under communism insured that it would acquire some distinctive Soviet 'cultural' features. The discouragement of individual initiative and a proclivity to emphasise weight of numbers in both manpower and equipment over qualitative technological factors were products of the communist period. Nevertheless, despite the sustained Soviet influence and control, the LWP also showed itself to be professional and able to exercise in practice a great deal of institutional autonomy within the Soviet harness. The Polish Armed Forces' strong institutional autonomy and identity within the Polish state provided a valuable starting point for its transformation into a post communist army.

DE-COMMUNISATION

The rapid collapse of communism in Poland in 1988-1989 heralded sweeping changes to the political, economic and social life of the country. The consequence of this change on the Polish Armed Forces was profound. No longer an instrument of Soviet security policy, the reborn Polish Army (*Wojsko Polskie*—WP) had to be transformed into a national institution and find a place in the new democratic order. Post-communist reform inevitably entailed radical changes to the personnel, force structure and mission of the Polish Armed Forces. Moreover, in the stringent post communist economic climate, slashing defence spending became a necessity for the transition to a market economy. The politics of transition also demanded the dismantling of the most objectionable features of the old order. As in the case of other compromised instruments of the former communist regime in Poland

Chapter One: Dismantling the Legacy of the Warsaw Pact

(police and security services), the armed forces went through an initial period of reform between 1989 and 1991 that aimed at eliminating elements and structures most closely associated with communist power in Poland.

For the Polish Armed Forces, de-communisation primarily meant the elimination of the Main Political Department (GZP) which institutionalised the connection between the Polish United Worker's Party (*Polska Zjednoczona Partia Robotnicza*—PZPR) and the armed forces. Through the GZP, party influence permeated the armed forces from top to bottom. In the party structure in the army, committees existed from the military district level to the regimental level with about 5000 committees of primary organisation reaching the smallest units.[5] Removing communist influence in the armed forces, however, did not simply entail changes to the organisational chart. Communist influence had to be measured in terms of personnel changes. In 1989, the scale of party affiliation was enormous and included:

- 92 per cent Officers
- 66 per cent Warrant Officers
- 40 per cent Non-Commissioned Officers (Professional)

When party membership is considered on the basis of position, 100 per cent of divisional, regimental and battalion commanders and 80 per cent of company and platoon commanders belonged to the PZPR.[6] The scale of party membership in the armed forces meant that a political solution to making the armed forces compatible with the new democratic political order presented some difficult alternatives for the first post communist governments.

For those in government, the challenge lay in determining which soldiers were loyal and trustworthy enough to the new political order to be kept and how many must go. One military commentator cut to the core of the problem facing the new post communist governments when he wrote: 'Regardless of the name, lustration, de-communisation, or verification amounts to questioning the loyalty of, and displaying confidence in, the cadres of the Polish Armed Forces'.[7] Although purging the armed forces in 1989-1990 was a necessary political task, it was not a simple military one. With the overwhelming majority of party members occupying leadership positions in the armed forces, if too many soldiers were dismissed or retired from service, then the political leadership gambled with the nation's security by drastically damaging the military capability of the armed forces. One Polish military analyst aptly described this risk:

> 'It is a complex process to renew the cadre structures of the army in such a way as to preserve the principle of competence at successive command levels. It calls for rational, long-term actions, and it takes time. The disruption of this process by a sudden verification, based on non-professional criteria, could actually become a surprising act of disarming ourselves by means of the actual elimination of army cadres for quite a number of years'.[8]

In the end, Poland's post-communist politicians opted for a selective and highly targeted de-communisation of the armed forces. The Main Political Department (GZP) was disbanded. On the eve of its liquidation, it numbered 7839 (5702 officers, 603 warrant officers and 1534 ncos). After a verification process, only 2192 transferred into a newly established military educational service. Party affiliations came to an end for all serving soldiers and the organisational 'apparat' disappeared. The elimination of the GZP was one of the most important acts of organisational de-communisation but not the only one.[9] The disbanding of the military secret police called the Internal Military Service (Wojskowa Sluzba Wewnetrzna—WSW) and the *Zarzad II* (2nd Department) of the General Staff (external intelligence) in 1990 eliminated the most independent and potentially dangerous elements of communist influence in the armed forces. Only about a third of the staff from them were selected for service in their successor organisations the Military Police (*Zandarmeria Wojskowa*—ZW) and the Military Information Service (*Wojskowe Sluzby Informacyjne*—WSI) which inherited both the counterintelligence and intelligence roles.[10]

Chapter One: Dismantling the Legacy of the Warsaw Pact

Apart from the dismantling of key party organisational structures with the attendant discharge from service of large numbers of their personnel, the highest ranking category of officers—the generals—underwent a thorough purge of their ranks. In April 1990, around 140 generals were on active service in the armed forces. By the end of 1990 the number of generals dropped by nearly one third to about 100.[11] Since 1991, the overall number of generals has been slowly creeping up from the 100 benchmark and by the middle of 1995 had reached 117 general grade officers.[12] The turnover of the number of generals from the communist period was in fact higher than the total numbers indicate. The newspaper *Polityka* in October 1992 reported that in the period 1989-1991 over a hundred generals left the army with only 24 new officers promoted to general rank.[13] What can be quite confusing is the fact that there are many more general grade posts than officers possessing the rank of general. For example, in 1991 there were 473 positions for generals in the armed forces with 349 of them occupied by officers with the rank of Colonel or Lieutenant Colonel.[14] Nevertheless, from the fragmentary and sometimes contradictory information that has appeared in the civilian and military press, it is clear that there has been an almost complete clearout of the most senior officers serving in the armed forces before 1989.

The question of personnel verification for the purpose of de-communising the Polish Armed Forces was not very systematic except for the categories of personnel discussed above. The early post-communist governments trod warily on this matter seeking a balance between de-communisation and continuity in military personnel. The reaction of the officer corps to the question of verification is in many ways central to this discussion. Military personnel, after all, are the ones most directly affected by policies designed to screen servicemen and determine whether or not they continue their military careers. The reaction of the officer corps if not enthusiastically in favour of a purge of its ranks was remarkably placid. The elimination of party influence and the promotion of an apolitical army that reflected 'national' rather than the ideological predilections of one political party was seen as a positive development.[15] Nevertheless, the question of 'verification' of members of the armed forces generated debate expressing a range of resentment. One former political officer cum education officer complained about the pariah status of officers most closely associated with the communist party apparatus. Another figure writing anonymously resented the role of civilians in the process: 'verification should be conducted by people who know the army and those who enjoy unimpaired moral authority—in principle, military men themselves'.[16] Still others regretted that there had not been a more thorough-going purge of the army.[17] On balance, discontent on the verification of 'cadre' in the armed forces has to be seen from the perspective of the wider national debate on purging institutions of communist influence. In this context, the verification process made sufficient progress in making personnel change and discharging those individuals most compromised by their allegiance to the old regime. It was a process aided by the massive personnel reduction prompted by the CFE (Conventional Forces Europe) Treaty and changing budgetary and military priorities (see discussion of manpower issues in next chapter). In the end, the military integrity of the armed forces remained intact after undergoing a massive culture change that was neither characterised by political score settling nor by preservation of the old order.

In addition to processes that dismantled old structures and shed unsuitable personnel, efforts were made to introduce new influences to the *Wojsko Polskie* in order to reflect the wider changes in Poland. The most visible of these cultural changes was the reintroduction of military insignia that preceded the communist period and efforts to revive aspects of military tradition discarded during communism. The re-adoption of the Polish eagle insignia with a crown, berets and shoulder patches on uniforms was evocative of those worn by the Polish forces in Britain during the Second World War. Institutionally, the creation of field ordinariates (Bishoprics) for the Roman Catholic Church in 1991 and Polish Autocephalous Orthodox Church in 1993 for meeting the spiritual and pastoral needs of service personnel represented a significant new input into the armed forces. In 1995, a military chaplaincy was established for Protestants in military service.[18] Previously, the Christian Churches faced serious obstacles to their work in the armed

Chapter One: Dismantling the Legacy of the Warsaw Pact

forces. Given the denominational composition of Poland, the Catholic ordinariate dwarfs that of the other Christian churches making it a dominant influence.[19] Church activity in the armed forces has provoked some criticism. There are officers who think that the Priest in uniform has replaced the political officer as a guide of ideological orthodoxy.[20] The discontent that has surfaced over alleged clericalisation, however, is not overwhelmingly present even among officers groomed under the pervasive influence of Marxist-Leninist ideology prior to 1989. The revitalisation of the influence of Christian churches on armed forces personnel serves an important role. It helps to reconnect the Polish military to the mainstream values of Polish society.

EVOLVING DOCTRINE

Parallel to the de-communisation process was the launch of a major revision of Polish security and defence thinking. In response to the changes in the post-Cold War security environment, Poland's 'defence' or 'military' doctrine underwent a fundamental change. In 1990 and again, in 1992, the Polish government published 'doctrinal' texts setting out the security and defence policy of Poland, the view of potential threats and the new purposes and tasks of the armed forces.[21] The Polish use of the term 'doctrine' encompasses a wide range of levels but, like its British counterparts, it represents a 'body of thought which underpins the development of defence policy'.[22] Two major documents have emerged since 1989 embodying the changes to Polish defence doctrine. The first was the 'Defence Doctrine of the Polish Republic' adopted in Spring 1990 and the second was the 'Security Policy and Defence Strategy of the Republic of Poland' officially accepted in November 1992. The former was clearly a first effort revision that still reflected some of the assumptions of the former communist regime, while the latter document that replaced it more definitively met the security desiderata of the new political order. The 1990 statement of doctrine still saw as an 'important element' Poland's 'membership in the Warsaw Pact'; the 1992 document made clear that 'Poland is striving towards Nato membership' (and the EU/WEU) as the central goal of its security policy.[23] Despite the fundamental shift in goals, there were significant elements in continuity between the two documents; both of them underscored the reassertion of national sovereignty that lay at the apex of defence doctrine. 'The strategic defence goal of the Republic of Poland', stated the 1992 document, 'is to uphold the nation's sovereignty, independence, and territorial inviolability'.[24] Overall, the 1992 document saw this goal realised in military terms by the national effort to maintain armed forces with credible capability and the attainment of membership in Nato.

The November 1992 document provided a military-strategic concept consistent with Poland's security policy goals to guide the transformation of the armed forces. At its core, it made the primary purpose of the armed forces the defence of the 'sovereignty and independence of the Polish nation'.[25] It also envisaged a secondary purpose in which the armed forces operated in coalition with other allied states either abroad or on Polish soil in support of international security. 'The Polish Armed Forces', stated the 1992 doctrine, 'must therefore be constantly prepared to form operational groups in order to fulfil various tasks as part of missions or expeditions by multinational allied armed forces'.[26] These definitions of the purpose of the armed forces stemmed from an assessment of the post-Cold War security environment that highlighted the 'atmosphere of uncertainty' prevailing in the region. The potential dangers stemmed from the internal upheaval attending the massive systemic transformation in the countries of the region and the existing and potential threats arising out of the instability found in the countries of the former Soviet Union. This amorphous threat environment led the authors of the 1992 statement of doctrine to define a 'defensive strategy' that did 'not assume the existence of a specific enemy or a specific scenario of military activity'.[27] Therefore, in meeting its primary purpose of defence of national sovereignty and independence in the ill-defined and unpredictable threat environment, the armed forces had to prepare for *tous azimuts* defence. The armed forces had to be prepared to meet a potential aggressor 'in any region of the country, in any direction and against any form of military threat'.[28] Although the 1992 document did not list conflict types, the document offered an implicit dichotomy in its discussion of responses to 'war . . . beyond a local conflict' and a 'conflict of lesser intensity'.[29]

The 1992 document broadly defined the force structure and tasks of the armed forces. The armed forces were to be structured into 'operational' and 'territorial defence' forces with each assigned the following tasks:

- 'The operational forces are prepared to fulfil the main tasks in wartime'.
- 'The territorial defence units support and secure the actions of the operational forces and independently carry out defensive and protective activity in their assigned areas of operations'.[30]

The document went on to define the tasks of each of the branches of the armed forces. The land forces were described as the 'core of the armed forces of the Republic of Poland'. Despite their pre-eminence, the 1992 document offered few specific tasks stressing in very general terms that the land forces were meant 'to repel an aggressor's land and airborne attacks through defensive action'. The Air Force and Air Defence Forces were described as maintaining the 'highest state of readiness during peacetime'. The tasks of the air force included the protection of Polish territory and the prevention of violation of Polish airspace. The navy's tasks were most clearly described and fell under the rubric of defence of the 'sea border' which included: protection of shipping, protection of economic interests in territorial waters and coastal defence (in conjunction with other branches of the armed forces). These general descriptions of tasks at least defined the roles of each branch and provided some basis to begin the transformation of the Polish armed forces.[31]

The 1992 defence doctrine was clearly written to serve in a transitional period. Its broadest aims illustrated its transitory character. It set out as its goals both the attainment membership in Nato and the preparation of an essentially re-nationalised defence posture. Membership in the Atlantic Alliance would force significant diversification away from the national *tous azimuts* military strategic concept while a failure to obtain a place in Nato would decisively reinforce an autarkic national approach. Such hedging may have been prudent in 1992 when Poland's prospects for eventual membership in Nato were still far from certain, but it presented a contradictory agenda from a military point of view. It has to be recognised, however, that the framers of the Polish defence doctrine laboured under the same security uncertainties faced by everyone in the early 1990s. In that sense they were no different than their British counterparts. The Statement on the Defence Estimates 1992 set out 'three defence roles' that emerged in that exercise postulated a similarly all-embracing set of objectives for the British Armed Forces to meet.[32] Subsequent statements of Defence Estimates did not substantially alter the three roles until the *Strategic Defence Review* (SDR) in 1998 confirmed what had been a gradually evolving move toward an expeditionary role for the British Armed Forces.[33] Incremental changes to British force structure, organisation and procurement in the 1990s suggested that a shift in emphasis had long preceded the actual redefinition of roles. Similarly, Poland has been shifting its force structure more in the direction of fitting into Nato while the 1992 doctrine still stands as official policy with its national *tous azimuts* objective.

From the perspective of 1998 with an invitation to join the Alliance in hand and the ratification process virtually complete, Polish defence doctrine looks in need of revision. A senior Polish officer has admitted that the 1992 doctrine was designed for a transition period and that evolving circumstances required that it 'should be changed'.[34] Discussion regarding the revision of the 1992 Polish defence doctrine is certainly underway in Polish official circles but no timetable has emerged for the publication and adoption of a revised statement. Drafting a replacement for the 1992 Polish defence doctrine is certainly underway in Polish official circles but no timetable has emerged for the publication and adoption of a revised statement. The discussion underway regarding the revision of the 1992 defence doctrine suggests the possibility of adopting something akin to the British 'mission types' first published in the 1993 White Paper. The Polish mission

Chapter One: Dismantling the Legacy of the Warsaw Pact

types being considered include: 1) total war, 2) regional conflict, 3) border incursion, 4) peace keeping, 5) peace enforcement and 6) providing relief from a natural disaster.[35]

Many of these categories suggest the possibility of deploying Polish forces outside national territory. The issue here is not the abandonment of the primary purpose of the armed forces to defend the 'sovereignty and independence of the Polish nation', but rather the degree of emphasis that will be placed on expeditionary tasks—particularly in the Nato framework. From General Robelek's point of view, the driver of local conflict had 'come to the forefront' and had distinct implications for the military strategic concept of Poland. 'The forces of Nato, as well as those of Poland which wants to become its member', stated Robelek, 'should thus be prepared for installing and sustaining peace in such situations'.[36] Poland's acceptance of Nato's military strategic concepts embodied in various post-Cold War documents will undoubtedly strengthen this shift in emphasis. The revised doctrine will undoubtedly contain at least an implicit recognition of a larger expeditionary role for the Polish Armed Forces. The process of revising the Polish defence doctrine will, like the British SDR, only confirm changes that have been long underway. In the Polish case it was driven by the goal of integrating Poland into Nato.

NOTES

1. The standard communist period history of the LWP is the massive *Ludowe Wojsko Polskie 1943-1945,* (Warsawa, Wydawnictwo MON, 1973). For a more critical account see Czeslaw Grzelak, Henryk Stanczyk and Stefan Zwolinski, *Bez mozliwosci wyboru: Wojsko Polskie na froncie wschodnim 1943-1945,* (Warsawa, Wydawnictwo Bellona, 1993).
2. The most detailed account of the role of Soviet officers in the Polish People's Army is Edward Jan Nalepa, *Oficerowie Armii Radzieckiej w Wojsku Polskim,* (Warsawa, Wydawnictwo Bellona, 1995).
3. Marek Henzler and Wlodzimierz Kalski, 'Wyjechali,' *Polityka,* 25 September 1993 and Maria Wagrowska, 'Problem wycofania jednostek bylej Armii Radzieckiej,' *Rzeczpospolita,* 24 February 1992.

4. See Paul C Latawski, 'The Polish Military in Politics,' in Jack Bielasiak and Maurice D Simon (eds.), *Polish Politics: Edge of the Abyss*, (New York, Paeger, 1984), pp. 268-292, Andrew A Michta, *Red Eagle: The Army in Polish Politics, 1944-1988*, (Stanford, Hoover Institution Press, 1990), and George Stanford, *Military Rule in Poland The Rebuilding of Communist Power, 1981 1983*, (London, Croom Helm, 1986).
5. Lieutenant Colonel Tadeusz Mitek, 'An Army Without Commanders,' *Polska Zbrojna*, 4-6 September 1992 in JPRS-EER-92-135, 22 September 1992.
6. *Ibid.*
7. *Ibid.*
8. *Ibid.*
9. Lieutenant Colonel Tadeusz Mitek, 'The Status of Military Reform,' *Polska Zbrojna*, 6-8 November 1992 in JPRS-EER-92-170, 17 December 1992.
10. Major Marek Ciecierski, 'Sluzby spejalne niejedno nosza imie,' *Polska Zbrojna*, 10 June 1996.
11. See Janusz B Grochowski, 'Who is to Defend the Security of the Country?,' *Zolnierz Rzeczpospolitej*, 9 May 1990 in JPRS-EE-90-080, 8 June 1990 and interview with Colonel Marian Stuglik, Deputy Chief of the Department of Personnel, Polish Ministry of Defence, *Zolnierz Rzeczpospolitej*, 11 July 1990 in JPRS-EER-90-130, 19 September 1990.
12. Numbers as of 22 May 1995 in *Wojsko Polskie: Informator '95*, (Warsawa, Wydawnictwo, Bellona, 1995), pp.413-419.
13. Interview with Zbigniew Skoczylas, director of personnel department, Polish Ministry of Defence, *Polityka*, 17 November 1992.
14. Stanislaw Lukaszawski, 'Report on the Status of the Military: Generational Sucession,' *Polska Zbrojna*, 22 April 1991 in JPRS-EER-91-085.
15. Lieutenant Colonel Tadeusz Mitek, 'A Non-party Military,' in *Zolnierz Rzeczpopolita*, 14 May 1990 in JPRS-EER-9-097 and Lieutenant Colonel Mitek, 'The Status of Military Reforms,' *Polska Zbrojna*, 6-8 November 1992 in JPRS-EER-92-170.
16. See Major Grzegorz Knasiak, 'Who Are We?,' *Zolnierz Rzeczpospolitej*, 3-5 August 1990 in JPRS-EER-90-137. Quotation taken from 'The Army Is Waiting,' *Po Prostu*, 8 November 1990 in JPRS-EER-91-006.
17. See interview with Colonel Stanislaw Dronicz in 'An Infected Army,'

Chapter One: Dismantling the Legacy of the Warsaw Pact

Tygodnik Gdanski, 30 June 1991 in JPRS-EER-91-110.
18. *Wojsko Polskie: Informator '95,* 139-142.
19. See interview with Brigadier General Slawoj Leszek Glodz, Field Bishop of the Polish Army in 'The Church Should Fill a Great Role in the Army,' *Przeglad Katolicki,* 1-8 March 1992 in JPRS-EER-92-050.
20. Marek Ciecerski, 'Pluton spiewa!' *Polityka,* 1 May 1993.
21. The terminology used expressing the defence doctrine can often be difficult to equate between countries as it may reflect national practices that do not easily translate into another country's conceptual system. The aim here is to be consistent and to reflect British and more broadly Western practices in terminology. For the sake of simplicity, Nato terminology will be avoided so as not to complicate the issue further.
22. *British Defence Doctrine,* Joint Warfare Publication, JWP) 0-01, (London, HMSO,1997), p.1.2.
23. 'Defence Doctrine of the Polish Republic,' 21 February 1990, in *Zolnierz Wolnosci,* 26 February 1990 in JPRS-EER-90-038.
24. 'Security Policy and Defence Strategy of the Republic of Poland,' 2 November 1992 in *Wojsko Polskie: Informator '95,* 16-32.
25. *Ibid.*
26. *Ibid.*
27. *Ibid.*
28. *Ibid.*
29. *Ibid.*
30. *Ibid.*
31. *Ibid.*
32. *Statement on the Defence Estimates 1992,* CM1981, (London, HMSO, July 1992), pp.8-9.
33. *The Strategic Defence Review,* CM3999, (London, The Stationary Office, July 1998), p.13.
34. Interview with Major General Marian Robelek, Deputy Cheif of the General Staff in 'Dylemat wyboru,' *Polska Zbrojna,* 2 January 1998.
35. Discussion with Polish Ministry of Defence officials September 1997.
36. Interview with Major General Marian Robelek, *Polska Zbrojna,* 2 January 1998.

CHAPTER TWO

PAINFUL BUT NECESSARY ADJUSTMENT: MANPOWER ISSUES AND INFRASTRUCTURE

Human resources are of paramount importance to the effectiveness of any military force. The most important issues facing the Polish Armed Forces as it moves into the new millennium concern its overall size, the composition and management of its serving personnel. Like many armed forces in Europe, central to the post-Cold War transformation of the Polish Armed Forces has been a long process of reduction in manpower. The cuts have been driven by a number of external and internal factors. The radically changed security environment in Europe, manpower ceilings stipulated in the CFE treaty and the curtailment of defence resources due to the pressing needs of Poland's transitional economy have all played a role in making manpower reductions inevitable.

Any manpower reductions, however, must be linked to some sort of vision for a remodelled Polish military. Determining the optimum strength of the post-Cold War armed forces is a problem that has a major long-term military and economic impact. The strength of manpower is intimately linked to force structure planning. Furthermore, manpower costs represent the single largest item of expenditure within the Polish defence budget and as such is an obvious target for tighter management. Lowering manpower costs has the potential for yielding additional resources to finance procurement programmes for modern equipment. With significantly lower manpower strengths, there is a similar knock-on effect to free up more resources by discarding surplus infrastructure unnecessary to the needs of smaller armed forces.

Chapter Two: Painful but Necessary Adjustment

Manpower issues are not limited to overall numbers. The composition of the armed forces and how its personnel are managed presents an even wider spectrum of challenges. Some of the problems to be confronted in terms of the personnel structure include determining the balance between conscripts versus military professionals and the numbers of officers versus non-commissioned officers. In addition, the management of military personnel requires that a host of social issues that directly effect the personal lives of members of the armed forces be addressed. Resolution of these issues cuts to the heart of the morale and military effectiveness of any armed force.

Such large-scale reductions and changes to career patterns are undoubtedly costly in human terms to Polish service personnel whose careers may be abruptly ended. From the point of view of the Polish defence budget, such fundamental change has its associated costs in the short to medium term as retraining, redundancy payments and pension outlays have to be found in the already limited financial resources. Manpower reductions and reform to the personnel structure, however, represents the most far-reaching and fundamental element of the Polish armed forces' adaptation to fit into Nato.

MANPOWER REDUCTIONS AND PERSONNEL STRUCTURE

In 1988, the manpower of the Polish Armed Forces numbered just over 400 000 men. Since then it has been undergoing a steady reduction. In the two years following the end of the communist regime, manpower was slashed by a quarter to around 300 000 men. Between 1991 and 1995, manpower totals stabilised in the vicinity of 280 000 men although there was a slight if perceptible reduction year on year. By 1996, however, it was clear from press reports that the reduced manpower levels of the first half of the 1990s did not mark the end of changes to manpower strength. Only in March 1997 was a decision reportedly taken to adopt a 'definitive' manpower model for the Polish Armed Forces.[1] From 1997 onwards, further reductions were launched toward an eventual strength of 180 000 men in 2004.[2] At present, the 180 000 level is official policy and the target date for achieving the manpower strength has been advanced one year to 2003 (see Fig 2.1).

FIGURE 2.1: COMPARISON OF MANPOWER AND EQUIPMENT HOLDINGS

	*1989/90	*1997/98	CFE LIMIT	Plan 2012 (Modified)	2012 Reduction on (Current CFE Limit)
Manpower	412 000	**241 750	234 000	***180 000	-54 000
Tanks	3300	1729	1730	1300	-450
ACV	3950	2135	2150	1380	-770
Arty (+100mm)	2090	1581	1610	1060	-550
Attack Helicopter	80	105	130	100	-30
Combat Aircraft	565	356	460	****230	-230

* Source: *The Military Balance* for the indicated year.
**Figure includes 17 000 navy personnel not included in CFE manpower limit.
***Strength by 2003
****Source: *Flight International*, 28 February-5 March 1996.

Chapter Two: Painful but Necessary Adjustment

Polish officials have not ruled out the possibility of a further reduction to 160 000. Budgetary considerations may prevail and force the adoption of the lower manpower ceiling.[3] Despite lingering uncertainty over the eventual manpower ceiling, something resembling a definitive policy has emerged concerning the manpower of the Polish Armed Forces.

A key component of the plan to reduce the overall manpower level is a design to adjust the structure of professional personnel to move it closer to models prevalent in Nato member states. Nato armies generally have personnel structures that reflect a pyramid with NCOs and enlisted ranks at the base with every decreasing numbers of officers as rank increases until the pinnacle is reached. The Polish structure inherited at the end of the communist period followed Soviet patterns and looked very different. The inherited structure of professional officers, warrant officers and NCOs resembles an inverted pyramid and if the enlisted ranks (conscripts) are added to the base of the pyramid, then it begins to resemble a barbell. To illustrate the structure, according to statistics published by the Polish Ministry of Defence, in 1994 the Polish Armed Forces had 89 500 professional service personnel. When broken down by rank category these consisted of 43 500 officers (49 per cent), 26 500 warrant officers (29 per cent) and 19 500 NCOs (22 per cent).[4] Three years later, some modest progress had been made in altering the structure but the inverted pyramid remained largely intact; the structure consisted of 41 051 officers (48 per cent), 28 432 warrant officers (33 per cent) and 16 155 NCOs (19 per cent).[5] Clearly there remain some considerable alterations to be made before the Polish armed forces possesses a personnel structure comparable to Nato armies.[6]

According to manpower projections for 1998 published by the Polish Ministry of Defence, by the end of that year the Polish Armed Forces would consist of 83 000 professional service personnel. When broken down by rank category it would have 39 400 officers (47 per cent), 26 000 warrant officers (31 per cent) and 15 600 NCOs (19 per cent).[7] The aim of Polish policy is to shift the personnel structure by

21

2003 to one consisting of between approximately 25 000-30 000 officers (30 per cent), 25 000-30 000 warrant officers (30 per cent) and 40 000-50 000 NCOs (40 per cent).[8] The projections suggest that up to 23 000 could be leaving the armed forces by 2003 as it is envisaged that the officer corps will consist of 30 per cent senior officers and 70 per cent junior officers.[9] Recently, the Polish newspaper *Gazeta Wyborcza* published figures comparing the present strength of the armed forces with the target for 2003. Although these figures do not entirely correspond to those of the aforementioned projections, they nevertheless are consistent with the general trend in restructuring of professional personnel:

CHANGES TO THE OFFICER CORPS[10]

Current Number	(1998)	Target for 2003
Generals	126	225
Colonels	2755	1125
Lieutenant Colonels	5736	3825
Majors	9648	2700
Captains	9451	6075
Lieutenants	5222	4725
Second Lieutenant	5657	3825

The biggest casualties in the process of restructuring personnel are going to be senior officers—majors, lieutenant colonels and colonels. Some 57 per cent are leaving the armed forces by 2003. The impact on junior officers will be less pronounced with 28 per cent leaving. The net effect of the personnel restructuring will be a dramatic cull of senior officers and a modest decrease in junior officers. The only category that will experience growth is that of the generals.[11]

For the non-commissioned professional personnel, there will be a sizeable increase in warrant officers and NCOs. The number of NCOs will more than double in number by 2003. The increased numbers of NCOs will be trained at existing officers' colleges in Poznan, Torun and

Chapter Two: Painful but Necessary Adjustment

Wrocław. In keeping with the larger role that NCOs are to assume in the Polish Armed Forces, the training syllabus will be substantial modified to bring it in line with NCO training in Nato countries.[12] The shift to reliance on NCOs to assume more leadership positions in the armed forces highlights a related problem in the Polish military—matching rank to position.

Accompanying the restructuring of personnel will be a re-grading of positions [*etatyzacja*] in the Polish Armed Forces. Currently officers hold military posts that in terms of responsibilities would be filled by an NCO or administrative posts normally filled by civilians in the armed forces of a Nato country. Likewise, there are some 400 posts for generals while the Polish armed forces possess around 130 actively serving generals. Colonels fill most of the general grade posts. The current Polish Defence Minister, Janusz Onyszkiewicz, has made it priority to eliminate at least half the number of general's posts and to conduct an armed forces wide reclassification of positions. In April 1998 the Polish Ministry of Defence launched the process of reclassification of posts with the full implementation of the process to be completed by January 1999. Changes in the permanent post structure will result in the reclassification of over 12 000 positions largely effecting senior officers who will essentially be out of a job.[13]

Apart from reversing the pyramid of professional service personnel and reclassifying positions, career patterns will also have to be altered if the Polish Armed Forces are going to be in line with practices in Nato countries. In the Polish Armed Forces, particularly in the army, professional soldiers often spent the bulk of their career in the same unit and base. The idea of rotation and changing jobs at frequent intervals common in Nato armies simply did not exist. This pattern has significant social consequences as housing, schools and amenities were organised on the basis of continuity of tenure at a given location. Moving to another base could mean leaving the family behind or loosing the assigned accommodation, as nothing might be available at the new posting.

The introduction of rotation in the most senior posts of the armed forces assigning them a three-year term of office was the most visible example of promoting personnel rotation and mobility. This high profile Presidential decision came on the eve of the Autumn 1997 parliamentary elections and caused a small political storm. The opposition parties, soon to become the parties of government, vigorously attacked the change. Remarkably the new Chairman of the Parliamentary Defence Committee stated that 'I believe that a term limit law will be a disservice to Poland'.[14] Suspicions about packing senior posts with officers sympathetic to the political left, given the timing of the decision and the rough and tumble of an election campaign, seems to have been behind the criticism. Despite the furore, no effort has been made by the new government to reverse the decision.

For the professional service personnel, uncertainty and job insecurity has been introduced into a profession hitherto considered very stable. With the large-scale reductions in manpower and the introduction of new practices since 1989, the professional soldier has had to cope with unprecedented change that inevitably effects morale.[15] The challenge of facing career adjustments is compounded by personal hardship due to dropping standards of living.[16] This problem particularly effects junior grade officers, warrant officers and NCOs. The cradle to grave welfare state of the old Polish People's Army is giving way to a new army of fewer benefits and a more cost conscious approach to spending. Professional soldiers are now required to contribute more to the cost of their housing.[17] Most damaging to morale, however, is a continuing shortage of housing. It is ironic that while the armed forces possesses barracks for double its present manpower it nevertheless suffers from a serious shortage of housing for the families of professional military personnel.[18]

Pay and the value of pensions has also been a significant issue for Polish military personnel. Military personnel are paid considerably less that their counterparts in Nato countries. According to Deputy Defence Minister Romuald Szeremietiew, a *Bundeswehr* sergeant makes as much as a deputy corps commander.[19] While the military pay scales are not comparable with Nato countries, in the Polish context, military personnel generally do well among state employees. Although there is a widespread perception in the armed forces that pay is too low, only staff in the security-intelligence services earn more than soldiers among public sector employees.[20] Despite the relatively good position among state employees, it is clear that many professional soldiers find it hard to make ends meet on their salaries. According to Deputy Defence Minister Szeremietiew, 20 per cent of career soldiers have second jobs and 30 per cent of all military families receive some social benefit.[21] The hardest hit are junior and non-commissioned officers. Onyszkiewicz, the Defence Minister, has targeted these ranks for equity pay increases and more money has been distributed to these least paid categories of service personnel.[22]

Retention of officers holding highly skilled military trades is a growing problem. With the Polish economy growing, computer scientists, electricians and communication experts can make more money in civilian life than in the armed forces. Fast jet pilots are leaving to earn more flying for commercial airlines.[23] Although such a retention problem is a familiar tale in many Nato member states, it is a relatively new phenomenon in Poland.

With so many officers leaving or having left the armed forces since 1988, the value of pensions has been a sensitive issue for some time.[24] The most recent furore concerning military pensions occurred soon after the new Polish government took power after the Autumn 1997 elections. The Government decided to bring military pensions in line with other public service employees. The reform potentially reduced the value of pension increases for retired members of the armed forces. It is clear that the Polish Defence Minister Onyszkiewicz and the Chairman of the Parliamentary Defence Committee were not enthusiastic about the project.[25] Reaction in the military was predictably angry.[26] There can be little doubt that this attempt to alter armed forces' pensions originated in the Polish finance ministry. A Presidential veto, however, stopped the project although the Government wishes to return to the issue again. No doubt it will tread more gingerly on what is a clearly a politically contentious issue.[27]

The cumulative effects of career uncertainty and the massive downsizing of the armed forces have taken their toll on morale. One indication of discontent is the emergence of a desire among serving officers for the setting up of a military trade union to represent the interests of professional soldiers.[28] The pressure surfaced in the Deans of the Officer Corps, an official structure of representatives in the officer corps that act as a safety valve and unofficial line of transmission of concerns in the officer corps. The response of Onszykiewicz was uncompromising:

> 'Trade unions are not necessary in the Army. Besides, the effective legislation prohibits them. . . . Trade unions may politicise the Army. They pose a significant threat. Traditionally, trade unions, even though they refrained from that at the beginning, have engaged in politics, and the Army should be kept far away from politics.'[29]

Onyszkiewicz, however, tempered this hard line by stressing that as defence minister one of his important roles was to defend the interests of the military. 'Since the Army is not represented by trade unions', he emphasised, 'it stands to reason that the minister speaks on behalf of the military'.[30]

There is one group in the armed forces that has a very limited representation by any measure. The role of women in the Polish armed forces is limited. There exist major barriers to increasing the number of women in the armed forces in a society that is conservative and traditional in its outlook. In a January 1992 interview, the then defence minister, Rear Admiral Piotr Kolodziejczyk, demonstrated the resistance in the armed forces to increasing the participation of women:

> 'To my mind, there is no room for a woman, a lovely and fragile being, on the brutal and cruel field of battle. Still, I perceive a niche for women in the armed forces. At present we have some 60 lady officers, chiefly in the medical service, but ladies could also serve in signal troops or monitoring services. . . I still cannot imagine that a 20-

Chapter Two: Painful but Necessary Adjustment

year-old girl in whom the maternal instinct might arise at the most unexpected moment could sign a contract for five years of regular military service.'[31]

In forces with a strength in excess of 200 000, in 1995 there were only around 100 women. By December 1997, this total increased to 143 women (139 officers and four warrant officers). These women serve in medical facilities and many of them appear to be highly qualified doctors.[32] In contrast, the British Armed Forces contained 14 831 women of all ranks in 1997 and approximately 70 per cent of all military trades were now open to them.[33] For the time being, women represent a negligible element in the personnel structure of the Polish Armed Forces. Polish society, however, is changing rapidly and the traditional roles of women are coming under pressure. Over time it is inconceivable that the armed forces of Poland will be immune from the wider changes in society that are expanding the role of women. At present, the armed forces is not prepared either in attitude or in meeting the practical challenges of having larger numbers of women in the military.[34]

PROFESSIONALS AND CONSCRIPTS

Poland, like so many countries following after the Cold War, is having to face the question of the professionalisation of its armed forces. General Jozef Buczynski, head of the Polish Ministry of Defence personnel department, noted in an interview in June 1998 that the emphasis on professionals is increasingly a military necessity: 'In the face of the dynamic development of military technology, military service is becoming a domain of professionals. In future, there will be no room in it for amateurs and undereducated soldiers'.[35] Military necessity in a democratic state, however, inevitably has to be reconciled with political and economic considerations. In Poland, economic considerations are undoubtedly a limiting factor behind the continued reliance on conscription.[36] Therefore, official policy has opted for making the Polish armed forces half-professional by 2003.[37]

Creating half-professional armed forces has meant that the personnel structure that has consisted of conscript and professional soldiers has had to be modified. This has led to the creation of a new category of extended service soldiers on contracts of differing conditions and lengths of service. The contract service can last up to five years and can be extended three times. The aim of this new category of military service is to entice able conscripts through financial incentives to extend their military service and become NCOs. It is hoped that eventually half of the enlarged NCO corps will be in the contract category.[38] The programme to increase the level of more professional service personnel has, however, suffered from the uncompetitiveness of the financial incentives. Like so many reforms, the effort to increase the number of contract soldiers has been constrained by resource limitations.[39]

Movement toward all professional armed forces also still lacks support among the Polish political leadership. The Polish President, Alexander Kwasniewski made clear his opposition to all-professional armed forces. 'National servicemen', stated the Polish President, 'bring fresh blood to the forces, preventing them from ossifying'.[40] The President's views on the value of conscription certainly correspond to the views of the current government's defence ministers who have argued that conscription underscores the duty of every citizen to contribute to the country's defence. Public perceptions, however, may be changing.

Since Poland regained its independence in 1918, conscription has been a central feature of its military manpower provision. Annually, around 300 000 young men of nineteen years of age are eligible for conscription with about 100 000 called up for military service.[41] In in the autumn of 1990, the length of service of conscripts was reduced from twenty-four months to the current eighteen months. A further reduction of length of service to twelve months has long been mooted and in the past year the Ministry of Defence signalled its intention of bringing in such a change by 2000. Since the parliamentary elections in Autumn 1997, the process has been accelerated. Members of the

Chapter Two: Painful but Necessary Adjustment

new coalition on the parliamentary defence committee have pushed for the reduction to twelve months to be introduced as soon as possible. The Ministry of Defence, however, has argued there are significant additional personnel costs entailed in a more rapid timetable for introducing the change.[42] Additional money would have to be found to cover higher intensity training, higher turnover of uniforms and increased discharge allowances. The overall costs were put at 111m zloty (US$30m).[43] Despite the preference of the Polish Ministry of Defence to delay the introduction of 12-month service, the decision was announced in May to move to the shortened term of service in May 1998. Apart from the additional costs, shorter service means that more men would have to be conscripted annually because of the more rapid turnover. The shorter service also means substantial changes to the training cycle. This in turn requires a reduction in the opportunities for deferment that allowed many, particularly the better educated, to avoid conscription.[44] Despite the issues to be resolved, the political debate, in any case, centred on the timing of reducing the length of military service and not its desirability. By November 1998, the government approved a bill shortening military service to 12 months from January 1999.[45]

The reduction in the length of military service may not be enough in the long run to meet changing public perceptions regarding national service. The frequent and well-publicised examples of the bullying of conscripts have not added to public popularity of national service. Despite military efforts to crackdown on bullying, it may be seen as one of the factors contributing to public disenchantment with conscription. Recent opinion polling by the Military Sociological Institute suggest that fewer young people want to serve in the armed forces and that many people view national service as a waste of time.[46] In May 1998, an opinion poll conducted by the CBOS organisation indicated that some two-thirds of those consulted support an all-professional army without conscripts.[47] The current system of conscription seems to provide many avenues for avoiding service for the more resourceful. Certainly the armed forces has been disappointed for some time by both the physical and mental abilities of is conscripts.[48] Conscientious objectors, ironically, find a more difficult path. Since 1988, Polish law has made provision for alternative military service for those conscripts whose religious or moral convictions preclude serving in the armed forces. The duration of alternative service lasts twenty-four months and is served in health, social welfare or public safety organisations. On an annual basis, however, less than 4000 individuals perform alternative service.[49] The system of military service in Poland faces a number of challenges. From the point of view of both the Polish public and the military, these may only be fully resolved by the complete professionalisation of Poland's Armed Forces.

REDUCING INFRASTRUCTURE

One of the major consequences of the dramatic manpower reductions was the problem of bloated infrastructure. With the armed forces roughly halved in less than a decade, there was clearly an enormous surplus of installations that went well beyond the requirements of the reduced manpower. To put the problem in perspective, the Polish Armed Forces anticipated a manpower ceiling of around 180 000 by 2004 but possessed in 1997 the capacity to house 300 000-400 000 military personnel. The physical assets of the Polish Ministry of Defence included:

- 258 garrisons and 1793 base complexes
- 299 000 hectares of Ministry of Defence land
- 190 400 hectares of firing and test ranges
- Garage space for 82 500 vehicles
- Storage space amounting to 3.3 million sq. m
- 55 airfields (47 hard-surfaced)
- 375 revetments for aircraft
- Airfield POL depots with a capacity of 130 000 cu m[50]

The problem of surplus infrastructure was compounded by the additional military facilities inherited from the former Soviet forces based on Polish territory. These facilities included:

Chapter Two: Painful but Necessary Adjustment

- Thiteen airfields
- One Naval base (Swinoujscie)
- Six Training grounds
- 70 400 hectares of land[51]

Only about 13 per cent of the facilities inherited from the Russians were taken over by the Polish Ministry of Defence. None of the airfields remain in military use and the vast bulk of the property reverted to the control of the State Treasury. The most substantial piece of infrastructure retained was the base and training facility at Swietoszow. It is estimated that it will take at least a decade before this facility is fully operational.[52] The condition of the military infrastructure acquired from the Russians is very poor. Any useable material was stripped from the facilities and what remained was often ransacked. The environmental degradation due to soil and water contamination found on the former Russian bases is a major obstacle to conversion to civilian uses. Although the cost of managing the disposal and clean up was assigned to special government programmes and not the ministry of defence, it nevertheless represented a further drain on the state budget.[53]

Although military infrastructure in Poland is huge, sizeable chunks of it are suffering from extensive depreciation or are in need of modernisation. Just staying still in terms of minimum maintenance represents a large drain on budgetary resources. The management of infrastructure is not simply about disposing surplus installations but it also requires investment and the development of new installations to meet current defence needs. For the Polish Ministry of Defence, however, the problem of affecting changes to its sizeable infrastructure will take some time. Since 1989, the Defence Ministry has been deactivating garrisons but not profiting from the disposal of assets.[54] The Ministry only established a property agency to manage its assets in the autumn of 1996. Under new budgetary rules, the proceeds from the sale of assets can be reinvested elsewhere in military infrastructure. The task of disposing unwanted assets has begun in earnest but the task faced by the property agency is enormous.[55] Into the new millennium, the agency will be shedding something like 35 per cent of the current infrastructure.[56] Deciding what facilities are to close and which ones are to be retained is not a simple matter. Closing military installations impacts on local communities and garrisons and can be as much a politically vexing issue in Poland as elsewhere.[57] Furthermore, the final shape and distribution of the force structure and its attendant manpower will be a major factor conditioning the disposal, modernisation or establishment of facilities. Similarly, the requirements of Nato in Poland will also influence decision-making on infrastructure.

The geographical distribution of Polish military infrastructure has been a major factor determining the establishment of Polish priorities in managing its physical assets. The bulk of the infrastructure for air and land forces is in the west of the country. For the air force this may not make any significant difference given the flexibility and endurance of aircraft, but for land forces the geography of military installations may require significant dislocation from present bases. Indeed emphasis on *tous azimuts* defence in the 1992 doctrine seemed to dictate a more even distribution of soldiers around the country. Defence ministry policy statements in the early 1990s anticipated a major shift in the stationing of forces over a period of a decade. In 1990, the distribution of forces was by zones 50 per cent west 30 per cent central and 20 per cent east. By 2000, the plan was to alter the stationing of forces to give them a more even distribution of 40 per cent west, 30 per cent central and 30 per cent east.[58] While the intended level of dislocation from west to east may be seen as necessary and desirable, such a shift did entail large expenditure on new infrastructure that would have to take place against the background of managing and disposing the large inventory of surplus installations.

Progress in dislocating forces in such circumstances has been slow. Moreover, there are indications that the dislocation of forces eastward may be scaled down and another approach taken. When interviewed in December 1997, the Polish Chief of the General Staff, General Szumski stressed that 'it is probably better to invest in mobility and combat effectiveness of our forces than new barracks and firing grounds.'[59] Such a course of action would do much to solve the cost

Chapter Two: Painful but Necessary Adjustment

conundrum of managing the costly maintenance and downsizing of surplus infrastructure while simultaneously making major investments in new facilities. It would allow the armed forces to upgrade relatively inexpensively the best of its installations in the west of the country. Moreover, from the wider view of government policy, it makes more economic sense spending money on upgrading Poland's road network, particularly its trunk motorways, rather than investing scarce budgetary resources into bricks and mortar on green field military installations. The accrued benefits not only meet national defence requirements by increasing strategic mobility but boost the Polish economy by putting into place much needed modern transport infrastructure. The problem of Polish military infrastructure is that there is simply too much of it. It is a significant 'vegetative cost' in terms of the Polish defence budget and requires radical pruning. Shedding unwanted installations, modernising the best of the existing physical assets and avoiding unnecessary and costly investment in new facilities offers a rational way forward regarding the development of Polish infrastructure. It must, however, be reshaped to meet not only national requirements, but also the infrastructure needs of the Atlantic Alliance.

NOTES

1. Pawel Wronski, ' KSORM on Changes in Armed Forces,' *Gazeta Wyborcza*, 14 March 1997 in: FBIS-EEU-97-073.
2. Pawel Wronski, 'Leaving the Army: Will the Polish Armed Forces Be Reduced by 50 000 Men over the Next Five Years?,' *Gazeta Wyborcza*, in: FBIS-EEU-96-065 and Polish News Agency (PAP), 16 April 1997.
3. See the testimony of the Janusz Onyszkiewicz, Minister of National Defence, to the Polish Parliamentary Defence Committee, 5 May 1998 and Major Ryszard Choroszy,'Przyspieszenie', *Polska Zbrojna*, 29 May 1998.
4. Tadeusz Mitek, 'Wojsko bez kadrowych tajemnic', *Polska Zbrojna*, 4 May 1994.
5. *The Polish Armed Forces—Illustrated Guidebook*, (Warsaw, Ministry of Defence Press and Information Office, 1997), p. 14.
6. Ryszard Choroszy, 'Odwrocona piramida', *Polska Zbrojna*, 6 June 1997.
7. Roscislaw Janoniuk, 'Budzetowe przymiarki,' *Polska Zbrojna*, 21 November 1994.

8. Major Ryszard Choroszy, 'Etaty i wakaty,' *Polska Zbrojna*, 15 January 1999. The figures given earlier in *Budzet MON 1997*, (Warsaw, Biuro prasy i informacji, 1997), p.23 fall into this range.
9. Choroszy, '*Przyspieszenie.*'
10. Pawel Wronski, 'Officers Stand at Ease', *Gazeta Wyborcza*, 21 September 1998, FBIS-EEU-98-265.
11. *Ibid.* and see interview with General Jozef Buczynski, *Polska Zbrojna*, 19 June 1998 and Z L, 'Armia przed wielkim manewrem,' *Rzeczpospolita*, 13 May 1998.
12. Tadeusz Mitek, 'Tablica na zakrecie', *Polska Zbrojna*, 11 September 1998 and 'Rewolucja przy tablicy?', *Polska Zbrojna*, 9 January 1998.
13. Choroszy, 'Przyspieszenie'; Interview with Janusz Onyszkiewicz, the Polish Defence Minister in *Rzeczpospolita*, 23 March 1998 and with Polish News Agency (PAP), 25 December 1997; and, Z L, 'Armia przed wielkim manewrem.'
14. See Polish News Agency (PAP), 30 September 1997 and Interview with Bronislaw Komorowski, *Rzeczpospolita*, 20 January 1998.
15. For example see Artur Golawski, 'Kolo fortuny', *Polska Zbrojna*, 15 May 1998 and two articles by Zbigniew Lentowicz, 'Kadra w ruchu' and 'Kamien polszlachetny,' *Rzeczpospolita*, 30 May 1996.
16. Tadeusz Mitek, 'Elita na kredyt', *Polska Zbrojna*, 4 September 1998
17. Zbigniew Lentowicz, 'Chorazowie biedy,' *Rzeczpospolita*, 8-9 February 1997.
18. The housing shortage has been an ongoing problem. See for example: Wieslaw Rasala, 'Regres mieszkaniowy takze w wojsku,' *Polska Zbrojna*, 3 March 1994.
19. Romuald Szeremietiew, 'Battle for Armed Forces,' *Wprost*, 7 June 1998 in FBIS-EEU-98-160.
20. Marek Henzler, 'Mnozniki do podzialu,' *Polityka*, 31 January 1998.
21. Szeremietiew, 'Battle for Armed Forces.'
22. Henzler, '*Mnozniki do podzialu*' and interview with Onyszkiewicz, *Rzeczpospolita*, 23 March 1998.
23. Z L, 'Officers Prefer Civilian Suits', *Rzeczpospolita*, 30 September 1998, in FBIS-EEU-98-274.
24. See for example '105 tys. Wojskowych emerytow i rencistow bez rewaloryzacji', *Rzeczpospolita*, 12 May 1993.
25. See interview with Bronislaw Komorowski and interview with Janusz Onyskiewicz, the Polish Defence Minister in Polish News Agency (PAP) 8 December 1997.
26. See Pawel Wronski, 'Will the Military Flee from the Military?,' *Gazeta*

Chapter Two: Painful but Necessary Adjustment

Wyborcza, 29-30 November 1997 in FBIS-EEU-97-335 and Pawel Wronski, Deputies and Generals on Funds and Pensions for Servicemen, *Gazeta Wyborcza*, 6-7 December 1997 in FBIS-EEU-97-343.
27. Interview with Bronislaw Komorowski.
28. Jerzy Jachowicz, 'Trade Unions in the Army,' *Gazeta Wyborcza*, 6-7 June 1998 in FBIS-EEU-98-167 and Zbigniew Lentowicz, 'An Independent and Self-Governing Soldier, *Rzeczpospolita*, 21 May 1998 in FBIS-EEU-98-142.
29. Quoted in Jachowicz, 'Trade Unions in the Army'.
30. Interview with Onyszkiewicz, *Rzeczpospolita*, 23 March 1998.
31. Interview of Rear Admiral Piotr Kolodziejczyk, *Wprost*, 12 January 1992 in JPRS-EER-92-015, 7 February 1992.
32. Edward Mazurkow, 'Podwojne powolanie', *Polska Zbrojna*, 8 March 1995 and report of Polish news agency PAP, 26 December 1997.
33. *UK Defence Statistics 1997*, Government Statistical Service, p.46 and Nigel Vinson, 'A Fairer Front-Line? The Role of Women in the Combat Arms', *RUSI Newsbrief*, November 1997, pp. 81-83.
34. Report of Polish news agency PAP, 23 November 1998.
35. Interview with General Jozef Buczynski, *Polska Zbrojna*, 19 June 1998.
36. Artur Golawski, 'Armia zawodowa?', *Polska Zbrojna*, 25 September 1998.
37. *The Polish Armed Forces—Illustrated Guidebook*, p. 21.
38. Onyszkiewicz interview by Polish News Agency (PAP), 25 December 1997 and *Zycie Warszawy*, 31 January 1997.
39. 'Nadterminowi na hustawce', *Polska Zbrojna*, 10 July 1998 and a more critial report in *Gazeta Wyborcza*, 15 April 1998.
40. Quoted on Warsaw Polonia TV, 30 June 1997 in FBIS-EEU-97-18.
41. Wojciech Modzelewski, *'Pacyfizm w Polsce,'* (Warszawa, PAN-ISP, 1996), p. 42.
42. See '12 miesi cy dla wszystkich,' *Rzeczpospolita*, 1 July 1994 and *Rzeczpospolita*, 4 February 1998.
43. Report Polish news agency PAP, 15 September 1998.
44. Interview with General Marian Robelek, 'Dylemat wyboru', *Polska Zbrojna*, 2 January 1998, Pawel Wronski, 'General Defence Duty: Shorter Service', *Gazeta Wyborcza*, 6 May 1998 in FBIS-EEU-98-126 and *Rzeczpospolita*, 20 November 1998.
45. Report Polish news agency PAP, 3 November 1998.
46. 'The Armed Forces, A Waste of Time?', *Gazeta Wyborcza*, 28-29 May

1997 in FBIS-EEU-97-153.
47. Renata Wrobel, 'Obowizek, ktorego latwo unikn', *Rzeczpospolita*, 22 May 1998.
48. Roman Przeciszewski, 'Embassassing Side of the Draft', *Polska Zbrojna*, 15 July 1992 and Zbigniew Lentowicz, 'Plagi na rekruta', *Rzeczpospolita*, 28 January 1995.
49. Modzelewski, pp. 43-45.
50. Ltieutenant Colonel Wlodzimierz Kaleta, *'Wiano armii,' Polska Zbrojna*, 23 May 1997, pp. 20-21.
51. Maria Wagrowska, 'Najwazniejsza sa lotniska,' *Rzeczpospolita*, 14 May 1997.
52. Wagrowska, 'Najwazniejsza sa lotniska.'
53. Katarzyna Zukrowska and Pawel Wieczorek, 'Conversion in Poland: The Defence Industry and Base Redevelopment,' brief 8, November 1996, Bonn International Center for Conversion.
54. Zbigniew Lentowicz, *'Demilitaryzacja Pultuska,' Rzeczpospolita*, 14-15 May 1994.
55. Report Polish news agency PAP, 24 November 1998.
56. Wieslaw Rozbicki, 'Cichy sojusznik wojska,' *Polska Zbrona*, 13 February 1998, p.22.
57. See Colonel Roman Przeciszewski, 'Fuzja troch nieelegancka,' *Polska Zbrojna*, 5 December 1997, pp. 34-36 and Lieutenant Colonel Wlodzimierz Kaleta, 'Kolobrzeg bez wojska,' *Polska Zbrojna*, 9 January 1998, p. 14.
58. Andrzej Karkoszka, 'Security Policy and the Armed Forces of the Republic of Poland,' in Jan Geert Siccama and Theo van den Doel, Restructuring Armed Forces in East and West,' (Boulder, Westview Press, 1994), p. 79.
59. Interview of General Henryk Szumski in 'Pokoj na wszystkich azymtach', *Rzeczpospolita*, 27-28 December 1997.

CHAPTER THREE
DEFINITIVE REFORM?: PLAN 2012

INTRODUCTION

The 1992 military strategic concept of Poland triggered a series of changes to the force structure, organisation and equipment priorities of the Polish Armed Forces. In the eight years following the demise of communism in 1989, most of these changes had the quality of dismantling something that existed before rather than building something new. It was on the matter of vision of the future that the 1992 document was most sparse on detail concerning the anticipated reform and modernisation of the armed forces. Only concerning the army did it give any direction indicating that it would consist of 'operational forces' and 'territorial defence forces'. The absence of a comprehensive plan, however, did not mean that no efforts at reform were made. Rather, the changes that occurred to the armed forces developed in a piecemeal fashion. General Szumski, the current Polish Chief of the General Staff confirmed this lack of a coherent approach to reform in this period:

> 'Our army has been in the process of reforms for many years now. Necessary as they were, those reforms were superficial, partial, and not based on a final vision. Separate segments were sorted out, while having in mind no complete picture of how the Army should look in the future.'[1]

There were in fact several attempts to introduce a comprehensive package of reform. The government under the premiership of Hanna Suchocka adopted 'Structure 1992' that aimed for armed forces possessing the equipment and manpower ceilings stipulated in the CFE treaty. Only in manpower levels did this plan have any hope of realisation. A project in the Presidential Chancellery dubbed 'Armed Forces 2010' attempted to bring a note of reality by attempting to match the force structure to the financial resources available but this 1996 effort never was a serious runner in terms of adoption as policy.[2] By Autumn 1997, however, the then Cimoszewicz government, made up of a coalition of former communist parties, launched with great fanfare *Tenets for the Programme of the Armed Forces Modernisation, 1998-2012*.[3] The 'Plan 2012', as it and its successors became known, was adopted as the definitive model for reform of the armed forces. The future of Plan 2012, however, was immediately called into question by parliamentary elections in the Autumn of 1997. The new coalition government to emerge after the election is made up of former Solidarity parties. Although the new government did not discard Plan 2012 it decided to review it and make necessary 'corrections'.[4] The most important correction it made was to take into account in the plan the requirements for integrating Poland into Nato.[5] Accordingly, the modernisation plan emerged with a new title: 'Programme for Integration into the North Atlantic Treaty Organisation and Modernisation of the Polish Armed Forces 1998-2012'. The alterations to the plan appeared to have been minimal in the end and the Buzek government confirmed the modified version as official policy.[6]

What all of the plans have in common is the shroud of secrecy, which has surrounded their gestation. The current Polish defence minister, Janusz Onyszkiewicz, has indicated that much of the reform plan will remain secret.[7] Even the recent discussion of Plan 2012 by the Defence Committee of the Polish Parliament was conducted in a closed session. The preparation of Plan 2012 involved an inter-ministerial working group and took a full year to draft. Although critics complained that it was the product of a small group in the Polish Ministry of Defence, in fact the process of drafting Plan 2012 encompassed many key ministries and the President's Chancellery.[8] The current Chief of the General Staff, General Szumski, has been involved in several of these efforts to produce a comprehensive reform plan for the Polish Armed Forces. His participation indicates that there was at least

Chapter Three: Definitive Reform?: Plan 2012

a strong element of continuity in the broad features of these successive plans even if some detail has undoubtedly changed.[9] Although the planning process has been enveloped in secrecy and nothing has been published that resembles the comprehensiveness and openness of the British *Strategic Defence Review* (SDR), it has to be recognised that a great deal of Plan 2012 has been officially revealed, albeit a slice at a time. From the many pieces it is possible to put together a picture that allows the official vision of the future of the Polish armed forces to be examined and critiqued.

There is no secrecy surrounding the reasons as to why a comprehensive and perhaps definitive vision for the Polish armed forces for the first quarter of the next decade has not emerged sooner. Although some may have attributed this slow process of creating a definitive military reform model to the lack of political will and judgement of successive governments, in fact of far greater consequence were major policy hurdles difficult for any government to control let alone predict. The reasons for the unhurried emergence of a 'final vision' in the 1990s can be attributed to two major factors. The most important was the scarcity of financial resources. The economics of transition made the fragmentary nature of military reform virtually inevitable. The domestic requirement for economic transition to a market economy entailed budget cuts and a major redirection of state resources away from defence spending. Put simply, the blank cheque defence spending of the communist era was no longer economically sustainable or politically possible. The priority of successive governments was to reduce the burdens of defence spending which left little room for additional resources to be invested in a radical restructuring of the armed forces. Apart from the scarcity of resources, the lack of a clear perspective on Poland's strategic goal of membership of Nato made it difficult to formulate a final vision of what the armed forces should eventually look like. The dilemma was embodied in the contradictory goals of a Polish defence doctrine that simultaneously postulated membership in Nato and provision for an autarkic *tous azimuts* national defence. The criteria for designing a force structure for collective defence in a coalition framework or one strictly for defending the national homeland are not identical. The Polish invitation to join Nato in July 1997 eliminated the uncertainty of gaining membership in the Atlantic Alliance as an inhibition to comprehensive reform of the Polish Armed Forces. The economic constraints, however, still remain to condition any comprehensive military reform.

SOMETHING OLD, SOMETHING NEW: MILITARY REFORM TO 1997

Throughout most of the 1990s, the Polish Armed Forces underwent incremental reform. The accent of this transitional period was on dismantling the parts of the force structure no longer relevant to post-Cold War conditions and taking the first steps toward a new force structure. The downsizing of manpower (see chapter 2) and the disbandment of a large number of superfluous military units were indicative of the gradual move away from Cold War era force structures. Among the more significant steps taken to adjust the armed forces to the new post-Cold War circumstances was the decision to dislocate units eastward. With the bulk of Polish forces stationed in the west of the country in 1990, the decision was taken to relocate a number of units to the eastern regions. By the year 2000, a more even distribution would be achieved increasing the percentage of units in the central and eastern parts of the country.[10]

The most significant early step to remodel the armed forces was the creation of a new Kraków military district in September 1991. Carved out of the existing three military districts, this new fourth district occupied the southeastern quadrant of Poland. The importance of the Krakow military district extended well beyond contributing to the more even geographical distribution of the Polish armed forces. The new military district became a laboratory for change, in particular to the army's force structure.[11] Unlike the existing military districts (Pomerania, Silesia and Warsaw), the force structure emphasised brigades rather than divisions as the principal units. The only exception was the 25th Air Cavalry Division (*Dywizja Kawalerii Powietrznej*—DKP). Ironically, the subordinate formations of this completely new division were based outside the Krakow district in central Poland near Lodz.[12]

Chapter Three: Definitive Reform?: Plan 2012

The military command structure of the Polish Armed Forces had the General Staff at its apex. Below the General Staff were four military districts with each containing a corps equivalent. The military districts served both administrative functions for the units based in their boundaries and provided a corps headquarters. They resembled self-contained fiefdoms within the command structure. The major formations in the Polish armed forces amounted to a total of eleven divisions and a handful of independent brigades. The divisions included one armoured cavalry, one air cavalry and nine mechanised.[13] Manpower levels in this period were approximately that of the CFE limit. Given this manpower ceiling, most of these divisions were in all probability under-strength and a few them amounted to little more than ghost units. Equipment levels in the armed forces were either at or below the Treaty Limited Equipment (TLE) limit of CFE (see Figure 2.1 in chapter two).

The only major innovation beside the creation of a fourth military district was the creation of a Land Forces Command (*Wojska Ladowe*—WL) in early 1997. Although it began virtually from nothing, the Land Forces Command took over many of the roles hitherto assigned to the General Staff. It was the beginning of a far-reaching reorganisation of the land forces that would eventually see most of the assets of the military districts subordinated to it. Administration and logistics remained under the control of the military districts with operational functions handed over to Land Forces Command. It was clear that up to the end of 1997 that developments concerning the Land Forces Command were far from over and that they formed part of an ongoing reorganisation of the command structures of the armed forces.[14]

Apart from a general shift from a regiment to a brigade structure throughout the Polish armed forces, the other major force structure innovations included the formation of the 25th Air Cavalry Division. Subordinated to the Krakow military district, this new formation located in a cluster of bases near the city of Lodz. Established during the course of 1994, this new division is the core of a new rapid reaction force. From its bases in the centre of Poland, its immediate reaction element was meant to deploy to any part of Poland within 24 hours. The 25th DKP's original structure had three subordinate regiments and at full strength around 150 helicopters.[15] Its initial start up cadre came from the elite 6th Air Assault Brigade. Despite the fanfare attending the inauguration of the air cavalry division, financial austerity in the Polish defence budget meant that finding the resources to obtain its full complement of helicopters receded into the distant future. Another factor threatening the development of the division was a conceptual debate over whether an airmobile or air mechanised model should be adopted by the armed forces. Some of this discussion questioned the need for having both an air cavalry division and an airborne brigade.[16] By Autumn 1997, the air mobile division was to be re-designated a brigade which better reflected the reality of its scale.[17] Other light forces that made their debut in Poland included two mountain brigades: the 21 Highland Rifle Brigade (*Brygada Strelcow Podhalanskich*—BSP) and the 22 Mountain Infantry Brigade (*Brygada Piechoty Gorskiej*—BPG) formed by 1994.[18] All of these changes were important but they did not amount to a comprehensive pattern of reform. For the most part, they represented new innovations grafted on to the previously existing force structure.

PLAN 2012: LAND FORCES

The introduction of 'Plan 2012' in Autumn 1997 postulated more comprehensive changes to the structure of land forces. Some elements integrated changes that had already taken place that were outlined above or refined them. However, for the first time something resembling a comprehensive approach to designing a future force structure emerged. The military district, hitherto a ubiquitous feature of the Polish Army in the twentieth century were destined for elimination with significant consequences for the command structure of the armed forces. Before 1997 most of their operational functions had already shifted to the Land Forces Command. Effective at the beginning of January 1999, the military districts were reduced to two: the Pomeranian in the north (incorporating the Warsaw district) and the Silesian in the south (absorbing the recently reconstituted Krakow dis-

Chapter Three: Definitive Reform?: Plan 2012

trict).[19] In the future the remaining military districts are likely to disappear. Their administrative and logistic functions will be taken over by the Land Forces Command and new provincial (*wojewodztwo*) administrative headquarters tied to territorial defence units (see below).[20] Answerable to the Land Forces Command are three corps: two mechanised with headquarters in Bydgoszcz and Wroclaw and an Air-Mechanised Corps with its headquarter in Krakow. The number of serving soldiers is planned to be at 107 000 men. It is possible that further downsizing could result in the number of soldiers being in the range of 90 000-95 000.[21]

Plan 2012 envisages a substantial smaller force structure. About half of the eleven divisions that existed in the mid-1990s were scheduled to be amalgamated or disbanded. By halving the number of divisions, Plan 2012 would leave the Polish Army with six, presumably less hollow, divisions and five independent brigades.[22] The 25th Air Cavalry division was redesignated a brigade, which better reflected the unit's actual strength.[23] The 22nd Mountain Brigade, one of the new units established since 1989, was to be disbanded with its cadre possibly forming the core of a new territorial defence brigade.[24] The Air Mechanised Corps being set up will consist of five independent brigades: one armoured, one mechanised, the Highland Rifle Brigade (Mountain warfare trained), the Air Cavalry Brigade and the Air Assault Brigade. Attached to the Air Mechanised Corps will be supporting artillery and engineer units.[25] The anticipated total number of combat brigades thus number 23 including eight armoured, twelve mechanised, and three light ones: air cavalry, air assault and mountain.

Although these changes to the Polish Army's force structure represent a major reduction in the number of major formations with a concomitant lessening of the hollowness of the surviving formations, the Plan 2012 army force structure nevertheless retains the equivalent of seven divisions. For an army whose strength is anticipated to be 107 000 men, it is clear that the hollow forces problem has not gone away and that many divisions will remain heavily cadre-ised and effectively 'reserve' divisions. By way of comparison, the post-SDR British Army has a roughly comparable strength in manpower but is planning to field only two deployable divisions. With the exception of the 11th Armoured Cavalry Division and the 12th Mechanised Division that are clearly first line units, the remaining four Polish Army divisions may effectively have one full strength brigade with two at highly reduced states of readiness.[26] Therefore, the number of brigades enjoying reasonable effectiveness will be much lower and perhaps in the vicinity of ten or twelve armoured or mechanised brigades out of the twenty envisaged in Plan 2012. Given continuing hollowness of many of the six divisions, might there not be a case for further rationalisation? The size of the force structure is tied to the retention of conscription and the reliance of reservists to fill out divisions in the event of a major conflict. Certainly, if the Polish Army were to become fully professional over time, then the size of the Plan 2012 force structure would undoubtedly be revised downwards. Similarly, if its manpower ceiling is lowered to between 90 000 and 95 000 men, then further reductions in the number of divisions would seen inevitable.

TERRITORIAL DEFENCE

Although the 1992 military strategic concept of Poland said little about force structure, it did postulate the creation of a new element—territorial defence forces (*obrona terytorialna*—OT). The development of OT forces, however, has moved very slowly until recent years. The reasons for the slow movement in creating territorial defence forces have been an ongoing disagreement over their size, role and importance in terms of defence priorities. Within the Polish Ministry of Defence, the dominant school of thought has seen the OT forces as a distraction; something that takes both time and resources away from more important issues related to the modernisation of operational forces. Indeed the brown beret OT units have been regarded as second class formations and disparagingly called the army up to '100 millimetres', a reference to the fact that these units will not field weapons larger than that calibre. One officer serving in an OT unit complained about prevalent attitudes in the army toward territorial defence: 'It is a matter of mentality and old habits. We are still seen as a mechanised

Chapter Three: Definitive Reform?: Plan 2012

infantry that can be used to bridge gaps in stationary defence or reinforce operational reserves'.[27] Both inside and outside the Polish Ministry of Defence, however, territorial defence has had its proponents.

Apart from officers serving on territorial defence staffs or units, the National Defence Academy (*Akademia Obrony Narodowej*—AON) has been the strongest advocate of the creation of a system of territorial defence. Its members certainly have had a significant role in spearheading the conceptual discussions, which have surfaced in the military press.[28] Not surprisingly, the staff officer responsible for developing territorial defence, Brigadier General January Komanski, has endorsed the concept in repeated interviews and articles in the military press.[29]

Recently, advocates of territorial defence have acquired a very valuable political ally in the Deputy Defence Minister, Romuald Szeremietiew. Szeremietiew is uniquely equipped to support the building of territorial defence forces. He attended the AON where he completed a dissertation on territorial defence systems. Before joining the defence ministry following the parliamentary elections in Autumn 1997, Szeremietiew argued in favour of territorial defence forces which he defined as 'a mass component of the Armed Forces based on the trained reserves and used to defend an area of soldiers' place of residence'.[30] He has since continued to support the development of territorial defence forces in his official capacity although his enthusiasm has attracted some criticism.[31] There can be little doubt, however, that Szeremietiew has instilled new life into efforts to build territorial defence forces.

The first territorial defence unit to be formed was the 1st Territorial Defence Brigade (*brygada obrony terytorialnej*—BOT) in January 1995 in Gdansk. To date, two others followed: 2nd BOT (Minsk Mazowiecki) and 3rd BOT (Zamosc). A third brigade might emerge based on the 22nd Mountain Infantry Brigade in Silesia.[32] During peacetime, the brigades serve a training bases of approximately battalion strength. One publication suggested a wartime strength of around 3800 for OT brigades that would be armed with light weapons, mortars and anti-tank guns. OT regiments (probably battalion strength) might include more specialist units such as engineers, military police and chemical warfare protection.[33] Eventually, OT units might gain hand-held anti-tank and anti-aircraft weapons. At present, the quality of equipment available to OT units is very poor.[34] The roles envisaged for territorial defence forces are twofold: in wartime to defend localities and key facilities and secure lines of communication, and to provide logistical support.[35]

In the development of territorial defence forces in Poland, a number of important questions are in the process of resolution: How large should territorial defence forces be and how do they fit into a broader military command structure? The peacetime strength of the current OT forces stands at about 5000 men with a wartime expansion to around 50 000 men. Szeremietiew advocated a peacetime strength of between 10 000 and 50 000 with a wartime strength of 300 000.[36] It seems that a ceiling of 10 000 OT troops in peacetime has been decided by the Polish Ministry of Defence, which would suggest a wartime strength of about 100 000.[37] The manpower strength may have been the result of political compromise between the differing camps within the Polish Defence Ministry competing for the limited resources available for force structure changes and modernisation of equipment.

How OT forces relate operationally to other land force elements is another question largely dependent on the command structure. This debate has not centred on whether OT units should be subordinated to higher levels of command (corps or land forces HQ) but over the geographical extent of a middle tier of command. Should the geographical scope of this command tier be military districts (covering roughly 50 per cent of Poland) or based on the existing 16 provinces? The demise of the military district and the recent reduction of the number of provinces have addressed this question. Clearly the OT units identification with a particular province or district is seen as a key element in the success of the emerging territorial defence structure.[38]

Chapter Three: Definitive Reform?: Plan 2012

During the course of 1998, a special taskforce headed by Deputy Minister Szeremetiew in the Polish Ministry of Defence formulated a revised model for the OT system.[39] The revised model of the territorial defence system envisaged a development in two stages a structure consisting of eventually 17 brigades (one for each province and one for Warsaw) and numerous battalions:

PLANS FOR TERRITORIAL DEFENCE FORCES

Land Forces	2003	2012
Brigade OT	11	17
Brigade Pontoon Bridge	4	4
Battalion OT	19	48
Battalion Engineers	8	8
Air Force		
Security Battalion	5	5
Fortification Eng. Battalion	2	2
Navy		
Companies OT	5	5
Coastal Observation Battalions	4	4
Security Battalion	4	4

The development of this OT structure will emphasise establishing units in the eastern part of the country first and also to create new OT units based on disbanding operational units. The adoption of a 12 month conscription programme has not resolved the practical problems of the interface of OT units with the training cycles of the operational forces. How long conscripts will spend with an OT unit is a major training question that still remains to be resolved.[40]

The success of the taskforce in producing a revised blueprint for territorial defence was not only due to a strong political impetus. An often cited advantage of territorial defence forces is their lower cost.

One Polish article gave figures that the cost of an OT battalion was 21 times less than a mechanised battalion and 42 times less than an armoured battalion. The infrastructure costs are also significantly lower.[41] Lower costs, however, do not necessarily mean effective defence on the cheap. The efficacy of territorial defence depends on how it relates to the other parts of a national defence system. That question cannot be answered until Poland's territorial defence forces reach a more developed stage.

PLAN 2012: AIR AND AIR DEFENCE FORCES

The Polish Air and Air Defence Force (*Wojska Lotnicze i Obrony Powietrznej*—WLOP) faces the most straightforward process of transformation of any branch of the armed forces. Organisationally, the major changes were initiated in the early 1990s, leaving the WLOP's combat aircraft divided between a northern 2nd Air Defence Corps (*Korpus Obrony Powietrznej*—KOP) headquartered in Bydgoszcz and a southern 3rd KOP headquartered in Wroclaw. The c150 combat aircraft that are operational are divided between three tactical aviation brigades—BLT—(a wing-sized unit) possessing ten squadrons—ELT—(*eskadry lotnictwa taktycznego*). The units will be based on 27 airfields out of the 55 military airfields in existence. Poland was unique in the Warsaw Pact, and now in Nato, as a user of specially prepared stretches of highway as dispersal airfields. WLOP plans on retaining nine highway landing strips (*drogowy odcinek lotniskowy*—DOL) for operational use with two of them new-built in the eastern portion of the country which lacks air bases.[42] Future plans for the air force anticipate a reduction of manpower to about 38 000 men by 2003 and 230 aircraft in the WLOP inventory.[43] Although WLOP has made considerable changes to adjust to post-Cold War realities and the needs of Nato membership a number of acute problems remain.

The foremost problem is the obsolescence of large portions of its inventory. As early as 1991, the Polish press was concerned about the material condition WLOP. 'Polish military aviation is basically obsolete' lamented one commentator.[44] The most modern aircraft opera-

Chapter Three: Definitive Reform?: Plan 2012

tional are Su-22s acquired in the second half of 1984 and Mig-29s received in 1989. The original batch of Mig-29s was supplemented by an additional ten aircraft acquired from the Czech Republic in a barter deal.[45] In 1999, only 77 Su-22s and 22 Mig-29s will be operational. The remaining numbers will be made up of about 50 Mig-21s of various versions and two Mig-23s that will reach the end of their service life soon after the turn of the century. When the fact that Poland's ageing An-26 aircraft and Iskra fast jet trainers are in need of replacement, then the scale of the problem of block obsolescence can be seen. Early next century, WLOP will require several new aircraft types to maintain a satisfactory level of capability. The requirement for the introduction of a new multirole aircraft is at the centre of Plan 2012 devoted to WLOP.[46] The only two technological bright spots have been the introduction of modern Nato compatible Identification Friend or Foe (IFF) systems, new air defence radars and an Air Sovereignty Operation Centre (ASOC) becoming operational on 12 February 1999.[47]

The obsolescence of the WLOP inventory coupled with an austere financial climate has had its impact on aircrew. Most pilots only average 55 hours per year against the Nato standard of 180 hours.[48] In addition the Polish Air Force has suffered a number of tragic accidents with the loss of aircrew. A spate of Su-22 crashes in 1995 led to a special commission being set up to evaluate the safety of the aircraft.[49] The most recent crash was on Polish independence day on 11 November 1998. An Iskra jet trainer crashed on a weather reconnaissance flight killing its two crew members. The incident caused a political furore and renewed questions regarding standards of safety given the low number of flying hours of pilots and the lack of money available for maintenance.[50] The net affect of these problems has been to see the departure of pilots from the airforce not only for reasons of poor morale but also seeking better pay and conditions in the civil sector.[51] It would be too much to say that the Polish airforce is in crisis, but until new aircraft are acquired the WLOP will continue to struggle to maintain a viable force structure.

Plan 2012: Navy

The poorest relation in the modernisation process is clearly the Polish Navy (*Marynarka Wojenna*—MW). It is the smallest of the three branches of the armed forces with about 17 000 men serving in the navy including 9000 conscripts. Its force structure of around 70 vessels has as its principal units three submarines, a guided missile destroyer, a frigate, seven corvettes, 15 fast attack craft or patrol vessels and 22 mine warfare units. These ships are organised into three major groups: 3rd Flotilla Gdynie-Oksywie, 8th Flotilla Swinoujscie/Kolobrzeg and the 9th Flotilla at Hel. In addition, the Polish Navy has a dedicated aviation component the Naval Air Arm (*Lotnictwa Marynarka Wojenna*—LMW) that operates a mixture of mostly aged fixed wing and rotary aircraft from three main bases: Babice Doly, Siemirowice and Darlowo.[52] The biggest problem facing the MW and its air arm is the need to replace obsolete ships and aircraft. Large numbers of ships date from the 1960s and 1970s with a smaller proportion dating from the early 1980s. Ironically, the most modern units are five Lublin class LST/Minelayers whose amphibious role ended with the demise of the Warsaw Pact. The submarine force nicely illustrates the material situation of the Polish Navy. A single modern Kilo boat built in the 1980s serves alongside two ancient Foxtrot boats laid down in the 1960s.[53] The LMW is in a similar condition operating Mig-21s that have no naval strike capability and Iskra training aircraft pressed into reconnaissance role.[54]

Before the adoption of Plan 2012, modernisation plans have gone through several versions. With each new version, the Polish Navy's ambitions have been pared further. The Navy has had to fit its modernisation plan to the availability of resources as its funding is likely to be the most limited among the three services.[55] Under Plan 2012, the major naval combats would consist of the following units:

- Two Submarines (one added after 2002)
- Six to seven Multipurpose Corvettes
- Seven Missile Boats (three with new missiles)

Chapter Three: Definitive Reform?: Plan 2012

- 23 Mine warfare units (five new; three SLEP)
- 12 Patrol craft

The aim is to complete a balanced fleet through limited new acquisitions and upgrades of the most modern units. The acquisition of a new submarine (probably a used one) has the purpose of maintaining submarine capability at a minimum level.[56] Earlier plans envisaged a submarine force of four to six boats which clearly was unrealistic in the resource climate that was likely to prevail.[57] Other elements in the modernisation programme seek the acquisition of command, control and communication systems, a modern anti-ship missile, new torpedoes and mine countermeasure systems.[58] The naval element of Plan 2012 may face the most difficult prospect of realisation even if its authors have charted a realistic course for the Polish Navy.

REQUIREMENTS VERSUS RESOURCES: MODERNISATION DILEMMAS OF PLAN 2012

The changes to the armed forces envisaged by Plan 2012 entail considerable modernisation of equipment both in terms of new acquisitions and update programmes for existing equipment. The priorities for comprehensive modernisation were originally described in eleven broad areas:[59]

- Integrated reconnaissance and EW systems
- Automated communication and command systems
- Artillery and smart munitions
- Air defence equipment and weapons systems
- Anti-armour equipment and weapon systems
- Aircraft
- Helicopters
- Armoured fighting vehicles
- Soldier's individual equipment
- Ships and naval systems
- Ancillary equipment (wheeled transport)

The change in government in Autumn 1997 led to a revision of modernisation priorities. These original eleven areas were integrated with Target Force Goals (TFG) agreed with Nato.[60] The shift in priorities undoubtedly placed greater stress on C^4I interoperability issues over the purchase of new hardware. Nevertheless, the eleven broad areas of priority remain a useful measure of the Polish modernisation needs even if accession to Nato has placed more importance on some of them.

Polish official estimates of modernisation costs have been in the vicinity of $10bn. Other estimates have suggested modernisation costs in the range of $11-19bn.[61] There is an underlying consistency to these published estimates and even the higher ones may simply reflect a wider range of official options. All of these estimates usually separate those costs associated with reaching minimum compatibility with Nato (C^4I priorities) and long-term modernisation programmes. The various estimates indicate that about $1.26bn would be spent on reaching minimum compatibility with Nato and $9bn to 2012 on modernisation programmes.[62] How does this estimate of $9bn, however, compare with the cost of specific items on the programme of modernisation?

The Polish government has not published a list of specific programmes for acquiring new equipment or updating existing stock. Obtaining accurate and consistent information is not possible. Figure 3.1 is a summary of specific programmes or areas that that have been discussed in the press or have come to light in official statements. Where possible, estimated costs for specific programmes have been included or estimates based on similar types of equipment procurement elsewhere in the world. The data for modernisation programmes in some cases lacks any cost estimates and in other cases cannot be defined with more precision due to a range of options that can effect costs. In short, Figure 3.1 can only give a rough perspective that underestimates overall costs. It nevertheless can give us a useable snapshot of costs associated with acquisitions and updates. A tally of the estimated costs of the programmes indicates a figure of $10bn, which roughly corresponds to the figure given above.

Figure 3.1 Modernisation: Requirements and Costs

Category	Requirement	Number	Options	Estimated Cost
Air Force				
	Multirole Aircraft	60-150	F-16 A/B C/D F/A-18 A/BC/D Gripen Mig-29 Mirage 2000	$1.2-3.5 bn Leasing $100m 12, 18, 36 US aircraft
	Mig-29 Upgrade Su-22 Upgrade	22	Dasa	$4.4 m
	Advanced Trainer /Light Attack	40 24	PLZ Mielec·I-22 Irdya (17 m-96 version; 11 upgrade, 6 new) Bae Hawk 100 Aero Vodochodny L-139 Surplus Alpha Jets	21 Hawk-100 cost Aust $640m
	Light Transport	12	CASA CN-235 Alenia G222 Alenia/ Lockheed Martin C-27J Refurbished surplus C-130s	$228m
	Long-range Anti-Aricraft System	?	Patriot PAC-3	13 Patriots w/761 missiles cost Saudi Arabia $1.03 bn

Chapter Three: Definitive Reform?: Plan 2012

Figure 3.1 continued

Category	Requirement	Number	Options	Estimated Cost
Army				
	T-72 upgrade to PT-91 Twardy standard	140	Bumar	$535 m Unit cost $3.8m
	BMP-1 Upgrade	c600	?	?
	Wheeled APC	300	?	?
	BRDM-2 Upgrade	471	?	?
	155 mm artillery (Turret for T-72 chassis)	94	VSEL/GEC AS 90 Wegmann PzH2000 Kerametal A-40 Zuzana	$300m ($2.8m per unit)
	LOARA SP AA System	?	?	?
	ATGW	5000	Israeli NT-D/HOT/Hellfire	$600m for helicopters/land forces
	Lorries/Light Vehicles	?	?	?
	Helicopters			
	Attack Helicopter	24	Apache Mangusta Super Cobra Tiger	$1.78bn
	Transport Helicopters	24	Armed Sokol	
Navy	Ships, aircraft and other			Z5bn ($1.25bn)

54

Chapter Three: Definitive Reform?: Plan 2012

If one assumed that the purchase of a new multirole aircraft would be funded outside the defence budget then that would cover uncosted items indicating that the Polish estimate of roughly $10bn remains credible. Although the parameters of estimated costs could be assumed to be close to $10bn, can the Polish defence budget provide resources in the period to 2012?

Polish defence spending since the end of communism has fallen in real terms but has stabilised between 2.5 and 3.0 per cent of GDP by the late 1990s yielding roughly $3bn per year.[63] This amount devoted to defence is not likely to change much making the conservative assumption that growth in the Polish economy, may be somewhat reduced by global economic conditions precipitated by developments in Asia. Additional resources for modernisation will have to be found within the defence budget. The planned reductions in manpower are aimed at decreasing personnel costs and shifting resources toward increased procurement. Resources for procurement are projected to steadily increase after 2003 until they reach approximately one-third of outlay in the Polish defence budget.[64] Assuming that for nine years (2003-2012) about one-third of the defence budget could be devoted to procurement, something like $1bn per year could be yielded. The roughly $9bn available for spending could optimistically just cover the spending programmes envisaged under plan 2012. More realistically, however, the shortfall between modernisation requirements and resources available might be as much as one-quarter or one-third of the overall estimated modernisation costs. This resource gap means that some procurement programmes would have to be deferred or capabilities and manpower pared further.

NOTES

1. Interview of General Henryk Szumski, *Polska Zbrojna*, 2 May 1997.
2. For a good summary of Polish attempts at comprehensive military reform see Krystian Piatkowski, 'Polish Special Forces—In Search of a New Posture', Conflict Studies Research Centre G60 February 1998.
3. See for example: 'Armia 2012', *Polska Zbrojna*, 12 September 1997,

Wojciech Luczak, 'Wojsko XXI wieku', *Zycie Warszawy*, 10 September 1997, Z L, 'Armia mniejsza i silniejsza', *Rzeczpospolita*, 10 September 1997, and Pawel Wronski, 'Armia XXI wieku, *Gazeta Wyborcza*, 10 September 1997.

4. 'Armia 2012 do korekty (?)', *Polska Zbrojna*, 26 December 1997, 'Armia 2012 do poprawki', *Polska Zbrojna*, 6 March 1998, and 'Armia 2012 poprawiona', *Polska Zbrojna*, 12 June 1998.

5. Janusz Zemke, 'Urodzaj na programy', *Polska Zbrojna*, 13 March 1998.

6. Report of Polish news agency PAP, 13 July 1998.

7. See 'Nadrabianie czasu', *Polska Zbrojna*, 24 July 1998.

8. Interview of General Henryk Szumski, *Rzeczpospolita*, 27-28 December 1997.

9. Interview of General Henryk Szumski, *Polska Zbrojna*, 2 May 1997.

10. Andrzej Karkoszka, 'Security Policy and the Armed Forces of the Republic of Poland', in Jan Geert Siccama and Theo van den Doel (eds.), *Restructuring Armed Forces in East and West*, (Boulder, Westview Press, 1994), p. 79.

11. Stanislaw Zajac, *Z dziejow Krakowskiego okregu wojskowego*, (Warsaw, Wydawnictwo Bellona, 1995), pp. 106-112.

12. Jerzy Sadecki, 'Nowoczesne, szybkie wojsko', *Rzeczpospolita*, 21 November 1994.

13. Eugeniusz Jendraszczak, 'The Structuring of the Polish Armed Forces in a Defensive Strategy', *The Journal of Slavic Military Studies*, 8 (December 1995), pp. 752-759, Andrew A. Michta, *The Soldier-Citizen: The Politics of the Polish Army after Communism*, (London, Macmillan, 1997), pp.50-62 and *Wojsko Polskie: Informator '95*, (Warsaw: Bellona, 1995), pp. 55-95.

14. Interview General Zbigniew Zalewski, *Jane's Defence Weekly*, 15 January 1997, Major Jaroslaw A Kopec, 'Formowanie ladowych', *Polska Zbrojna*, 2 May 1997 and 'Ladowa formacja w nowej szacie', *Polska Zbrojna*, 5 September 1997; Report Warsaw TV Polonia Network, 20 November 1997 in FBIS-EEU-97-324.

15. Lieutenant Colonel Wlodzimierz Kaleta, 'Kawaleria', *Polska Zbrojna*, 23 May 1997, Stanislaw Lukaszewski, 'Wysilek i wielka przygoda', *Polska Zbrojna*, 8-10 April 1994, 'Polish Army Creates Rapid Reaction Corps', *Jane's Defence Weekly*, 2 July 1994, *Wojsko Polskie: Informator '95*, p.76-77 and Apolinary Wojtys, 'Etapami w nowoczesnosc', *Polska Zbrojna*, 30 June 1994.

16. Piotr Bernabiuk, 'Fantazja pod kontrola', *Polska Zbrojna*, 2 May 1997,

Chapter Three: Definitive Reform?: Plan 2012

Grzegorz Holdanowicz, 'Formacja pelna klopotow', *Polska Zbrojna*, 6 March 1998, Brigadier General Stanislaw Koziej, 'Wojska powietrzno-zmechanizowane', *Polska Zbrojna*, 20 September 1994 and Major Jaroslaw A Kopec, 'Rozpunkty widzenia', *Polska Zbrojna*, 29 August 1997.

17. Major Jaroslaw A. Kopec, 'Ladowa formacja w nowej szacie', *Polska Zbrojna*, 5 September 1997.
18. Zbigniew Damski, 'Czy mamy wojska gorskie?', *Polska Zbrojna*, 6 February 1996 and Jacek Milewski, 'Pod znakiem szarotki', *Polska Zbrojna*, 24 May 1995.
19. Reports of Polish news agency PAP, 1 December 1998, 23 December 1998, 28 December 1998 and 7 January 1999.
20. Report of Polish news agency PAP, 23 July 1998.
21. Wlodzimierz Kaleta, 'Pierwsi wsrod rownych', *Polska Zbrojna*, 19 February 1999.
22. See Artur Glowacki, 'Wygaszanie?', *Polska Zbrojna*, 13 February 1998 and Mariusz Vero, 'Remont kapitalny', *Polska Zbrojna*, 5 June 1998.
23. See 'New Structures for Ground Troops', Rzeczpospolita, 21 December 1998 in FBIS-EEU-98-356 and Hubert M. Krolikowski, 'Poland battles "hollow forces" syndrome', *Jane's International Defence Review*, June 1997.
24. Mariusz Vero, 'Wielka przebudowa', *Polska Zbrojna*, 9 October 1998.
25. Jerzy Sadecki, 'Army: After the Dissolution of the Cracow Military District; First Corps', *Rzeczpospolita,* 8 January 1998 in FBIS-EEU-99-008.
26. This pattern was suggested in a meeting of the Parliamentary Defence Committee. See *Gazeta Wyborcza,* 27-28 March 1993.
27. As quoted in Zbigniew Lentowicz, 'Army Up to 100 Millimetres', *Rzeczpospolita*, 3 February 1998.
28 See for example Major. Krzystof Gasiorek and Colonel Ryszard Jakubczak, 'Wojska Obrony Terytorialnej—to przyszlosc polskiej armii (1-3)', *Polska Zbrojna*, 20-22 February 1995 and an interview with General Boleslaw Balcerowicz in *Gazeta Wyborcza,* 12 February 1997.
29. See the following contributions to the OT debate by Brigadier General January Komanski in *Polska Zbrojna*, 11-13 March 1994, 2 February 1995, 28 March 1997 and 28 November 1997.
30. Quoted from Romuald Szeremietiew, 'Poland's Defence Capability', *Rzeczpospolita*, 1 September 1997.
31. See Szeremietiew articles in *Rzeczpospolita* on 22 January 1998 and 19

June 1998. The controversial satirical magazine, Nie, has titled at Szeremietiew's interest in territorial defence. See *Nie* 5 March 1998.
32. Lentowicz, 'Army Up to 100 Millimetres'.
33. Jerzy Zielinski, 'Transformacja sil zbrojnych', in *Raport o stanie bezpieczenstwa panstwa—aspekty zewnetrzne*, (Warsaw, PISM, 1995), p. 91.
34. Lentowicz, 'Army Up to 100 Millimetres'.
35. Romuald Szeremietiew, 'Nato and National Defence: On the Need to Create a Territorial Defence System', *Rzeczpospolita*, 19 June 1998 in FBIS-EEU-98-173.
36. Report by Polish news agency PAP, 10 September 1998.
37. Report by Polish Radio, 26 February 1999.
38. Report by Polish news agency PAP, 11 January 1998.
39. 'Ruch w OT', *Polska Zbrojna*, 22 May 1998
40. Robert Rochowicz, 'Stara nazwa, nowa koncepcja', *Polska Zbrojna*, 9 April 1999.
41. Interview of Brigadier General January Komanski in *Polska Zbrojna*, 28 March 1997 and Tadeusz Mitek, 'Weekendowa armia?', *Polska Zbrojna*, 7 August 1998.
42. Taken from a trio of articles by Grzegorz Holdanowicz: 'Koniec i . . . poczatek oczekiwania', *Polska Zbrojna*, 29 August 1997, 'Kontriowersje na skrzydlach', *Polska Zbrojna*, 7 August 1998 and 'Polish Air Force A New Dawn', *Air Forces Monthly*, May 1999, 56-63.
43. Andrzej Jeziorski 'Poland to cut air force', *Flight International*, 28 February-5 March 1996 and Holdanowicz, 'Polish Air Force A New Dawn', *Air Forces Monthly*, May 1999, 56-63.
44. Lieutenant Colonel W Kaleta, 'The Wilting Wings', *Polska Zbrojna*, 5 September 1991 in JPRS-EER-91-151 9 October 1991.
45. Paul Latawski, 'Another Sale of the Century: Central Europe and the Multi-Role Aircraft Market', *RUSI Journal*, June 1997, pp. 51-52, p. 54 and Andrzej Przedpelski, *Lotnictwo Wojska Polskiego 1918-1996*, (Warsaw, Bellona, 1997), p. 295.
46. Miroslaw Cielemiecki, 'Holes in the Sky Will the Polish Air Force Survive Till the 21st Century', *Wprost*, 18 October 1998 in FBIS-EEU-98-289 and Holdanowicz, 'Polish Air Force A New Dawn', *Air Forces Monthly*, May 1999, 56-63.
47. Grzegorz Holdanowicz, 'Identyfikacja dla bezpieczenstwa', *Polska*

Chapter Three: Definitive Reform?: Plan 2012

Zbrojna, 30 May 1997 and 'Pajeczyna z importu', *Polska Zbrojna*, 31 July 1998 and John D Morrocco, 'New ASOCs Link Regional Airspace', *Aviation Week and Space Technology*, 22 March 1999.
48. Holdanowicz, 'Polish Air Force A New Dawn', *Air Forces Monthly*, May 1999, pp.56-63.
49. 'Commission to probe Polish air force Su-22 Fitter accidents', *Flight International*, 23-29 August 1995 and Kuba Spiewak, 'Wings of Disastor', *Warsaw Voice*, 6 August 1995.
50. Grzegorz Holdanowicz, 'Reanimacja', *Polska Zbrojna*, 7 February 1997 and Report by Polish news agency PAP, 12 November 1998 and 'Boj o nalot, boj o zycie', *Polska Zbrojna*,30 January 1998.
51. Report by Polish TV, 28 January 1998.
52. Poland entry in *Jane's Fighting Ships 1997-98*, (London, 1997), pp. 514-521 and Robert Rochowicz, 'Polish Navy and Programmes', *Naval Forces*, June 1998 and 'Stopa wody do Nato', *Polska Zbrojna*, 22 January 1999.
53. *Jane's Fighting Ships 1997-98*, The material condition of the Polish Navy has been the source of much discussion. See Lieutenant Colonel W Kaleta and Captain R Kowal, 'Zapominanie Baltyku', *Polska Zbrojna*, 26 June 1998 and Captain R Kowal, 'Marynarka na miare', *Polska Zbrojna*, 20 February 1998.
54. Grzegorz Holdanowicz, 'Odrzutowa pustka', *Polska Zbrojna*, 19 March 1999.
55. Kowal, 'Marynarka na miare'.
56. Rochowicz, 'Polish Navy and Programmes' and 'Stopa wody do Nato'.
57. Captain Robert Kowal, 'W morzu potrzeb', *Polska Zbrojna*, 17 October 1997.
58. Rochowicz, 'Polish Navy and Programmes'.
59. Major Ryszard Choroszy and Tadeusz Wrobel, 'Program modernizacji', *Polska Zbrojna*, 24 October 1997 and 'Eleven Paths to Renewed Polish Armed Forces', *Military Technology*, September 1997.
60. 'Poland's Place Within The Treaty', *Military Technology*, September 1998.
61. See the following sources: 'Arms Factories to be Privatised', *Rzeczpospolita*, 3 July 1997 in FBIS-EEU-97-184, Elzbieta Firlej, *Koszty integracji z Nato,* (Warsaw, DBM-MON, 1996) and 'Estimated Cost of Nato Enlargement', (Polish Euro-Atlantic Association, 1996).
62. The Firlej study cited above and based on Polish Ministry of defence esti-

mates is being used as the template.

63. *SIPRI Yearbook 1998: Armaments, Disarmament and International Security,* (Oxford, OUP, 1998), p.223, 229.

64. See Budzet MON 1997, (Warsaw, MON, 1997) and Ryszard Choroszy, 'Armia XXI wieku', *Polska Zbrojna,* 12 September 1997.

CONCLUSION

The transformation of the Polish Armed Forces since the end of communism has been a long and complex process that will continue well into the first decade of the new millennium. It also much be stressed that no military organisation ever achieves an optimum model. The ability to evolve constantly by assimilating new technologies and devising new doctrines for their employment is an ongoing challenge for any armed forces. Poland is no exception to this fact as it seeks to bring its armed forces to a standard comparable to its Nato counterparts. Such an undertaking, however, inevitably challenges the Poles to find the correct balance between commitments and resources in order to achieve a credible but affordable defence. How successful has Poland been in finding this balance in reforming its armed forces and what more needs to be done?

One area that still requires further work is the revision of the *defence missions* of the Polish Armed Forces. With Poland formally joining the Atlantic Alliance on 12 March 1999, the military-strategic concept drafted in 1992 is beginning to show its age. While Poland cannot be criticised for not doing this sooner as British defence missions evolved throughout the 1990s, the 1992 document needs to be replaced with something that offers more specific defence missions to guide the evolution of the force structure of the Polish Armed Forces. Of the key aims of Polish security and defence policy described in the 1992 document, one has been achieved (Nato membership) while the other (*tous azimuts* defence) is no longer relevant. The drafting of a new military-strategic concept would have to address the degree to which Poland intents to be a contributor to the Alliance's new missions. As these call for more mobile, flexible, deployable and sustainable forces, there are clear implications involved in determining the priorities in force structure development.

The area in which the Polish Armed Forces have achieved the

most difficult but necessary change is in manpower reductions and personnel restructuring. It is a process that is expensive both in human and financial terms and is an unavoidable precursor to force structure changes and modernisation programmes. The emergence of a final vision of the manpower parameters and rank structure has been an important development. It promises to mark a clear end to a process that began in the late 1980s and will carry on to 2003. While there may be more adjustments and possibly some slippage in the timetable for realising manpower adjustment plans, clearly this is a reform that is moving rapidly toward resolution. More problematic is the restructuring of the personnel structure to produce a new pyramid with fewer officers and more NCOs. Less visible is the source of all these new NCOs and the military education and training infrastructure to produce them. In addition, social problems experienced in the armed forces need to be addressed whether they concern housing shortages for professional cadre or addressing the bullying culture inflicted on conscripts. These problems will require continued efforts to improve the quality of experience for those serving in the armed forces. Despite these caveats, the changes to the manpower and personnel structure have gone a long way to laying a necessary foundation for moving forward with changes to the force structure and modernisation programmes.

Plan 2012, in its various guises, is a comprehensive attempt to design a new force structure for the Polish Armed Forces. For the land forces, Plan 2012 has included significant reductions (from eleven to six divisions) and considerable new innovations such as the development of an air mechanised corps and territorial defence forces. Although this force structure design represents a dramatic leap forward toward producing an army that is both realistic and effective given Poland's resource base, it perhaps is not bold enough. A further reduction of at least two divisions might be an adjustment that would further lessen the problem of hollow forces. Quality rather than quantity is the benchmark of capability in post-Cold War armies. The doctrinal and operational relationship of territorial defence forces to the main oper-

Conclusion

ational forces is an issue that is clearly in need of further development. While many important questions have been resolved such as a command structure based on Poland's new provincial territorial units, the question of fitting into a conscript's training programme service with territorial defence units still needs to be resolved.

The Polish Air Force is at a crossroads in terms of its aircraft inventory. The acquisition of a new aircraft in the beginning of the next century is a necessity if the air force is to retain viable operational capability. Unfortunately, the cost of acquiring a new multirole aircraft is likely to be the single most expensive and least affordable part of the Polish Armed Forces' modernisation programme. The recent interest of the Polish Defence Ministry in leasing options for Western aircraft, particularly American, may offer a way out of a resource versus capabilities *cul de sac*. It has its pitfalls insofar as leasing a particular aircraft type may make it difficult, if not impossible, to purchase a different aircraft. The likelihood of the Polish authorities moving ahead soon with a large purchase of a new a multirole aircraft and thereby burden its transitional economy is highly unlikely. The delay in moving ahead with a replacement aircraft is proof enough that Polish economic prudence prevails instead of procurement policies driven by national hubris or the persistence of Western arms suppliers.

The Polish Navy will have to make due with the smallest slice of any modernisation pie. Its plan for a balanced force is sound if somewhat ambitious. The biggest question must be the retention of submarine capability. Submarines are expensive weapon systems as is the attendant training infrastructure. Retaining one Kilo boat is simply not a viable option and another boat needs to be acquired to maintain operational capability. The high costs of seeking an interim second submarine or a new one would seem to be the most vulnerable aspect of the navy's modernisation plans to either deferment or abandonment. Over the long term, it would be probably better for Poland to buy into a future Danish, German or Swedish submarine replacement programme and share the spectrum of associated costs.

Poland has been criticised both abroad and at home for perceived shortcomings in preparing its armed forces for Nato membership. Whether the source of this criticism is the *Washington Post* or *Wprost*, similar problems are cited and most of them can be attributed to a lack of resources.[1] As discussed in chapter three, there is shortfall between the modernisation requirements and the resources that are likely to be available to meet them. Despite this likely shortfall, it is clear that the bulk of modernisation plans will be funded from the projected budget resources. It is the steady achievement of the greatest numbers of these modernisation goals that is crucial both to the future of the Polish Armed Forces and its utility to the Atlantic Alliance even if expectations are not met in full. Successive Polish governments have resisted the temptation of jeopardising the pursuit of sensible spending programmes to meet the needs of a transition economy by embarking on profligate and unsustainable levels of defence expenditure. This official realism in approaching the task of modernising the Polish Armed Forces was nicely summarised by the Deputy Defence Minister, Romuald Szeremietiew:

'There is no army in the world that would have exclusively ultramodern weapons. This results primarily from economic considerations. It turns out that it is cheaper to use older equipment to train soldiers. In line with standards in Nato armies, ultramodern equipment makes up 25 to 35 per cent of the entire armament. Poland should also reach this standard and, more importantly, it is able to reach it.'[2]

This realistic approach to modernisation is in line with Nato expectations. The Alliance has stressed the need to spend on personnel training and meeting key interoperability requirements rather than making investment priorities centre on expensive acquisition of new equipment.[3] The process of modernisation, it is understood in both Brussels and in Warsaw, will take at least a decade.[4]

It is unfortunate that the outbreak of the crisis in Kosovo, so soon after Poland's accession to Nato, as it only highlights the short-term limits to Poland's contributions to Nato rather than Polish long-term

Conclusion

prospects. Polish modernisation efforts need to progress more before Poland can make more than a token contribution to Alliance operations. It is clear that the deployment of more than a battalion of troops to the Balkans above and beyond the existing Polish deployments and commitments to SFOR in Bosnia, creates real strain on limited defence resources.[5]

Nevertheless, Poland has found the resources to express its solidarity by deploying elements of its elite GROM unit (the Polish SAS), a company from the 21st Highland Infantry Brigade to the Nato operation in Albania and a transport aircraft to aid the humanitarian relief operation.[6] No doubt if Poland were asked to make a larger troop deployment to contribute to a Nato ground operation in Kosovo, it would endeavour to find the necessary financial resources (Polish public opinion has been the strongest among the new members in supporting the Nato air campaign in the Balkans).[7] As long as such demands for larger deployments are not placed on the Polish government, however, Poland's contribution is likely to be guided by its means. From the perspective of Warsaw, by not indulging in short-term and unpredictably expensive commitments related to the Kosovo crisis, the modernisation of the Polish armed forces can proceed uninterrupted and in the long term add real value to Poland's contribution to the Alliance.

NOTES

1. *The Washington Post* article appeared on 18 March 1998 and prompted a swift rebuttal from the Polish Ministry of Defence. See reports by the Polish news agency PAP, 19 March 1998. For examples of criticism appearing in the Polish press see 'Jacek Bochenek, 'The Guard Duty; How are the Polish Armed Forces Prepared for Membership in Nato?', *Wprost*, 17 May 1998 in: FBIS-EEU-98-134, Wojciech M Darski, 'Under the Atlantic Treaty', *Tygodnik Solidarnosc*, 29 January 1999 in FBIS-EEU-99-034 and Witold Gadowski, 'With What to Nato?', *Gazeta Polska*, 28 October 1998.
2. Romuald Szeremietiew, 'The Polish Fist', *Wprost*, 31 January 1999 in FBIS-EEU-99-028.
3. See Frank Boland, 'Force Planning in the New Nato', *Nato Review*, Autumn

1998, pp.35-35, Javier Solana, 'On Course for a Nato of 19 Nations in 1999', *Nato Review*, Spring 1998, p.4 and Paul Mann, 'Nato Swings into Strategic Balancing Act', *Aviation Week and Space Technology*, 22 March 1999, p. 56.

4. See comments by the Polish Defence Minister, Janusz Onyszkiewicz in a report by the Polish news agency PAP, 5 May 1998 and Mann, 'Nato Swings into Strategic Balancing Act'.

5. See the remarks of Marek Siwiec the Head of the National Security Bureau, Polish news agency PAP, 19 April 1999.

6. See the following reports: TV Polonia, 13 and 22 April 1999 and Polish news agency PAP, 11 April 1999.

7. According to a CBOS opinion poll (conducted 8-15 April), 54 per cent supported the air campaign with 31 per cent against it. See *Gazeta Wyborcza,* 21 April 1999. A Demoskop poll (conducted 9-12 April) put those in favour of the air campaign at 63 per cent with those opposed at 22 per cent. See *Gazeta Wyborcza,* 17-18 April 1999.